# CENTURIES OF HANDS

*An Architectural History of
St. Francis of Assisi Church
and its Missions,
Ranchos de Taos, New Mexico*

and
The Historic American Buildings Surveys
of
St. Francis of Assisi Church
and
The Chapel of Our Lady of Talpa

## Van Dorn Hooker

*with*

*Corina A. Santistevan*

This project was supported in part
by a grant from the National Endowment for the Arts, a federal agency.

SUNSTONE
PRESS

SANTA FE

*Front Cover:* Front facade of St. Francis of Assisi Church, John Martin Campbell. Photographs of people working on the church by the author and from The Museum of New Mexico.

*Back Cover:* The apse, by John Martin Campbell.

First Edition

Printed in the United States of America.

10 9 8 7 6 5 4 3 2 1

Library of Congress Cataloging-in-Publication Data:

Hooker, Van Dorn, 1921–
    Centuries of hands: an architectural history of St. Francis of Assisi Church and its missions, Ranchos de Taos, New Mexico: the historic American buildings surveys of St. Francis of Assisi Church and the Chapel of Our Lady of Talpa/Van Dorn Hooker.
        p.   cm.
    Includes bibliographical references.
    ISBN: 0-86534-234-2 (paper)
    1. San Francisco de Asis Church (Ranchos de Taos, N.M.)—History. 2. Ranchos de Taos (N.M.)—Buildings, structures, etc. 3. Chapel of Our Lady of Talpa (Talpa, N.M.)—History. 4. Talpa (N.M.)—Buildings, structures, etc. I. Title.
NA5235.R3H66  1996
726′ .5′ 0978953—dc20                                                                95-4855
                                                                                    CIP

Published by  SUNSTONE PRESS
                    Post Office Box 2321
                    Santa Fe, NM 87504-2321 / USA
                    (505) 988-4418 / *orders only* (800) 243-5644
                    FAX (505) 988-1025

*Father Michael Patrick O'Brien, 1944–1993. Photograph by Vicente Martinez. Courtesy of Corina Santistevan.*

This book is dedicated to the memory of Father Michael O'Brien. Father Mike was pastor of St. Francis of Assisi Church from 1977 to 1982, during which time he inspired, researched and directed the reconstruction of the church both inside and out.

*The retablo by Molleno in the northwest transept. Photograph by John Martin Campbell. 1996*

# CONTENTS

## *FOREWORD*

4 October, 1990
Feast of St. Francis of Assisi
Church of San Damiano
Assisi, Italy

Pilgrims:

I am most grateful to Van Dorn Hooker for his interest in the San Francisco de Asis Church in Ranchos de Taos, New Mexico, U.S.A. Beginning with Fray José Benito Pereyro, O.F.M., and continuing to the present day Pastor, Fr. Johnny Lee Chavez, he presents a chronicle of the architectural history of the church.

Like the chronicle of a great Oak or Cottonwood tree, the rings measure the times and circumstances of the church and later parish of St. Francis. However, to see the tree and not the roots is to miss the real story and connection. St. Francis was built by the Franciscans and traces its roots and story back to San Damiano, the first church Francis repaired during his conversion.

To Francis of Assisi the church was to serve the people and was in fact the people. The story of Francis and the repairing of San Damiano is the heart and soul of the spirituality that has continued to inspire the people of Ranchos de Taos, Talpa, Llano Quemado and Los Cordovas/Cordillera. Each generation has responded to the call to "repair my church" and has followed the example and vision of Francis by rolling up their sleeves and opening their hearts to continue the work.

This book will provide a strong architectural and historical base for future pastors, parishioners and friends of this sacred place of celebration and worship.

May St. Francis and his love of God and all creation always be a focal point of the community's prayer and work. May the energy and blessing of Francis and Clare of Assisi inspire all who read and study this chronology of faith and love to continue in spite of the elements and the times this annual work of repair required by this unique living and breathing church.

May San Francisco de Asís Church never be entombed or memorialized to the point of becoming a museum, but may it be faithful to its roots and continue to be a simple ordinary church and a sacred place for all.

Special thanks to all the parishioners of St. Francis who it was my joy and honor to serve as Pastor from 1977 to 1982.

—Father Michael O'Brien

The beauty of the church lies in the
centuries of hands that have worked on it
with love and devotion.
                    —*An anonymous Taos artist*
                                    *1967*

Not being a writer or an historian but a retired architect, I have tried to record to the best of my ability what I have discovered about the architectural history of St. Francis of Assisi Church, with particular emphasis on what has happened to the church building since 1966.

When Monsignor Francis Reinberg, then Administrator of Temporalities for the Archdiocese of Santa Fe, called me in the autumn of 1966 and asked me to go to Ranchos de Taos with him to look at a construction problem at the church of St. Francis of Assisi I had no idea that it would spark such an interest on my part in this wonderful old church. I was then the university architect for the University of New Mexico and had my hands full with the problems of the burgeoning campus. The firm in which I was a partner in Santa Fe until 1963 had done numerous projects within the Archdiocese and, because Monsignor Reinberg and I had become good friends, I could not turn down his request. The church, unfortunately, had so many problems that a major remodeling and restoration project had to be undertaken in 1967. I followed the work, taking photographs and making occasional notes, until it was finished. I felt that such a major remodeling of this most significant structure, which is on the National Register of Historic Places, should be recorded for posterity.

Through the years I visited the church many times when I was in the Ranchos de Taos area. I watched the deterioration of the "hard plaster" and wrote an article about the 1967 work for the magazine *New Mexico Architecture*. Some time in the late 1970's, Father Michael O'Brien came by to see me at the university and we talked about the problems with the failing stucco and what to do about it. Again, I followed the 1979 remodeling to its completion and collected information about what transpired.

It seemed to me that since there was no comprehensive history of the church and since I had a great deal of information about its recent architectural history, I should add this to my records. After I retired from the university, I set about doing it, and became more and more interested in the whole history of the church. This led to additional research that I had not anticipated. I met many wonderful people who gave me help and encouragement, people who loved the church and wanted an accurate record of its architectural history.

There has been a great deal of misunderstanding about the age of the Ranchos de Taos church. Most writers thought the church was much older than later research has discovered. By citing recent references I hope to reinforce the 1813–1815 date for the construction of St. Francis of Assisi Church.

As the scope of my research widened I came to the conclusion that the history of the church was incomplete without a brief history of its plaza. The difficult part has been trying to distill the enormous amount of available material onto a few pages.

I had always been interested in the story of the Historic American Buildings Survey (HABS) work done in New Mexico in 1934 and 1940. John Gaw Meem and my former partner, Bradley P. Kidder, had told me a little bit about the HABS project and I had done some research on it. The measuring and recording of St. Francis church and the Chapel of Our Lady of Talpa were done in 1934, and some of the most interesting stories about the program were told by a member of the Talpa party. I have included a chapter on the HABS work on both buildings.

In another twenty years or so, depending on when the parishioners decide to celebrate, the church will be two hundred years old. I doubt that I will be around to participate in the celebration so I say, God bless you, St. Francis of Assisi Church, may you stand forever as a monument to the many hands that have tended you with love and affection through the centuries.

—VDH

# ACKNOWLEDGMENTS

So many people have helped me that I know I will omit some as I name them. If I do, I hope they will accept my thanks and apology. Foremost has been Corina Santistevan of Ranchos de Taos, the archivist for the church and a very active force in recording and preserving the history of the area. She has introduced me to people who know the history of the church whom I would never have been able to meet otherwise. She has found material for me, criticized my writing, edited the manuscript and become a very good friend.

Monsignor Francis Reinberg, now deceased, was an old friend I must thank for getting me involved with the church in 1966.

Father Michael O'Brien, Father Mike to everyone, spent much time telling me about the restoration work done under his guidance, and giving me good counsel.

Melissa Howard proof-read the manuscript and kindly corrected my mistakes, made suggestions and generally kept me on course.

George Smith Wright, FAIA, now Dean Emeritus of the School of Architecture, the University of Texas at Arlington, provided me with all of his office material on the 1967 remodeling. I have discussed the project with him many times.

M. Kent Stout and Stan Moore were architects in Wright's office and worked on the 1967 project. They have loaned me photographs and drawings and answered many of my questions. John Kessell, author and historian, director of the de Vargas project at the University of New Mexico, provided me with some of his research material, answered my questions and generally advised me.

Vicente M. Martinez, a photographer and associate curator of exhibits at the Millicent Rogers Museum in Taos, was most helpful with advice on which photographs to use.

Marina Ochoa, director of the Office of Historic-Artistic Patrimony and Archives of the Archdiocese of Santa Fe, has been most helpful in providing access to archival material.

Robert Nestor and Beverly Spears, who were with the firm of Johnson Nestor and did the studies leading to the 1979 restoration, told me much about that project and gave me copies of their reports.

Others who helped me in different ways were Sandra D'Emilio, curator of paintings at the Museum of New Mexico; Jan Dodson Barnhart, curator of the John Gaw Meem Archive of Southwestern Architecture at the University of New Mexico; Richard Rudisill, photography historian, and Arthur Olivas, photographic archivist, with the Museum of New Mexico; Alfred Regensberg and the staff at the State Records Center and Archives; Thomas Merlan, director of the Office of Cultural Affairs and State Historic Preservation Officer; Victor Grant and later Skip Miller, curator and associate director of the Kit Carson Historic Museums; the staff in charge of the Historic American Buildings Survey material in the Library of Congress; and my friend and colleague Jack (John Martin) Campbell, research professor of anthropology at the University of New Mexico, who made many photographs for the book and critiqued the manuscript.

A grant from the National Endowment for the Arts, for which I am most grateful, helped pay part of the expense of doing the research and collecting the photographs.

My special thanks to Nancy Meem Wirth for her support.

I thank my wife and fellow architect, Marjorie "Peggy" Hooker, who listened to me talk about the ongoing research, encouraged me and corrected the manuscript, and also my daughter Ann and son John who helped me struggle with the word processing.

—VDH

## CHAPTER 1— RANCHOS DE TAOS PLAZA

The origin of the name Taos is uncertain. There are many versions of its meaning such as the one T. M. Pearce gives in *New Mexico Place Names*. He says it is a Spanish approximation of Tewa Indian words, "tu-o-ta," red willow place, or "tua-tah," down at the village.[1] This is disputed by some contemporary residents. Historically, Taos Pueblo was referred to in Tiwa, their language, as "the place at Red Willow Canyon."[2]

The present-day community of Ranchos de Taos was called by different names, but the most commonly used was Las Trampas de Taos, literally The Traps of Taos because of the many beaver traps set in the nearby Rio de Las Trampas. In the 1765 will of Francisco Xavier Romero it is called "este paraje de San Francisco de las Trampas en la Jurisdiccíon del Valle de San Gerónimo de Thaos" (this place of San Francisco de las Trampas in the jurisdiction of the Valley of San Gerónimo de Taos). Later on, the eighteenth-century settlement received the appellation "El Rancho:" "El Rancho de Nuestro Padre San Francisco del Rio de las Trampas." After the plaza was completed, the term "el puesto" (the outpost) was often added to the name of the place: "El Puesto de Nuestro Padre Seráfico Francisco del Rancho de las Trampas," indicating the quasi-military function of the plaza.[3]

It has been the opinion of some archaeologists that the Taos Valley was first occupied around 900 A.D. However, recent archaeological surveys and excavations have discovered many Archaic campsites which indicate a much earlier occupation. The Archaic period is defined as being between 6000 B.C. and 750 B.C. That the Anasazi settlement was in place by 900 A.D. is confirmed by ruins of room blocks that have been found in the Taos area.

Around 1100 A.D. is the first indication of population aggregation with the building of larger pueblos of 50 to 100 rooms. The large Pot Creek Pueblo dates from 1175 to 1200 A.D. It is the oldest pueblo in the valley known to have a defined plaza with a large ceremonial kiva. It, like others such as the Hondo Pueblo in the Arroyo Hondo Valley and possibly Cornfield Taos or Picuris Pueblo, may have been settled by people who had previously lived in small, dispersed villages.[4] Cornfield Taos was occupied between 1325 and 1400 A. D. The present Taos Pueblo was occupied around 1400 A.D. soon after Cornfield Taos was abandoned.[5]

The valley and the pueblo were first visited by Hernando de Alvarado, an officer with the Coronado expedition, in 1540. Because the valley was so verdant compared to much of the surrounding area, it was attractive to the Spanish settlers who began to arrive around 1600. One of the primary objectives of the Spanish was to bring Christianity to the Indians, but early attempts with the Taos people were not too successful.[6] When Juan de Oñate established the first permanent Spanish settlement in New Mexico near present San Juan Pueblo, in 1598, he assigned Fray Francisco de Zamora as missionary to the Taos area.

Hostility of the Taos Indians to white domination soon arose. In 1609, Oñate was accused of killing a young Taos leader by hurling him from a roof. In the same year an alliance was reported of Taos and Picuris with the Apache and Vaquero against the Spanish. Part of the difficulty arose from the attempt of religious authorities to prohibit native rites and from civil authorities demanding tribute. In 1613 an open revolt against the payment of tribute resulted in Governor Pedro de Peralta sending troops to the pueblo. Fray Alonso de Benavides, in his visitation of 1627, noted that the resident priest, Tomás Carrasco, was building a church in spite of great difficulties.

Friction between the Spaniards and Taos Indians continued until January, 1640, when the Indians killed their priest, Fray Pedro de Miranda, and other Spaniards in the vicinity, destroyed the church and fled northward to the Cuartelejo Apache. They returned about twenty years later, and the conflicts began once more. The collection of tributes continued, but a much more serious problem was the beginning of Spanish encroachment on lands the Indians considered tribal possessions.

The Pueblo Rebellion of 1680 began in the Taos Pueblo when Popé, the leader of the rebellion, decided that Taos was the place from which to plot the uprising. From Taos he sent runners to the other pueblos telling the time for the revolt to begin. When it started, on August 10, 1680, some seventy settlers as well as two priests were killed near Taos by the Indians. They then joined in the taking of Santa Fe. The Taos Indians resisted the re-establishment of Spanish rule after the reconquest by General Don Diego de Vargas in 1692, not submitting until 1696 after several campaigns by de Vargas. By the turn of the century they had resigned themselves to cooperate with the Spanish in mutual defense against the attacks by the Comanches and Utes.[7]

By the middle of the seventeenth century there were some friendly Apaches, some Plains Indians and mixed-blood Indians living together with the Spanish in the valley. The area where Ranchos de Taos came to be located is on the Cristóbal de la Serna land grant. It had originally been granted to Fernando Durán y Cháves before the Pueblo Revolt. Although the grantee, his son Cristóbal and Sebastián de Herrera were the only Spaniards to escape from the Taos Valley during the revolt, they did not return after the reconquest and thereby lost title to their grant.[8]

In April, 1710, the Fernando Durán y Chavés grant was awarded to a soldier, Captain Cristóbal de la Serna, who was stationed at the pueblo. There is no evidence that he settled the land, but he may have used it for grazing livestock. Serna was killed in the ill-fated Villasur Expedition to the Platte River in 1720 to look for suspected French invaders. The troops were decimated in an attack by a band of Pawnees and French.[9] His sons, Juan and Sebastián de la Serna, sold the land on August 5, 1724, to Diego Romero, and Acting Governor Juan Paez Hurtado revalidated the grant to Romero on November 24, 1724. Diego Romero was the son of Alonso Cadimo and Maria de Tapia, workers on the hacienda of Felipe Romero at Sevilleta, south of Albuquerque.[10] Romero was known as "El Coyote" because of his mixed Spanish and Indian ancestry. The large Romero family were the first non-Indian settlers on the Serna Grant. Romero himself settled on the northern boundary of the grant, the Rio de Don Fernando, closer to the pueblo. His son, Francisco Xavier Romero, alias El Talache (the mattock) appears to have been the first settler upon the Rio de las Trampas, establishing his hacienda, "Talachia," there in the 1730's. He was not alone in the valley for the area was the ancestral home of certain clans of the Taos Indians and continued to be utilized by the Indians in the colonial era. Archaeological remains and documentary evidence indicate Indian settlements near the present site of Ranchos de Taos on the river well into the eighteenth century. A settlement of friendly Jicarilla Apaches, who professed an interest in Christianity, was established on the river in the 1720's. By mid-century small numbers of "Genizaros," mostly detribalized Plains and Taos–Plains mixed-blood Indians, had settled in the area.

By the 1760's there was a community made up of these people plus the "Coyote" families and several Spanish families. This community, Las Trampas de Taos, by 1765 was already dedicated to St. Francis of Assisi. The ranches of the settlers were spread along the waterways close to the arable lands rather than being clustered into defensible plazas. Each hacienda, located on sizable acreage, tried to provide for its own defense with fortifications such as walls and towers. However, a severe Comanche attack in 1760 and succeeding raids forced the settlers by 1770 to abandon their homes and return to the security of the pueblo.[11]

In 1760, Bishop Pedro Tamarón y Romeral, of Durango, was making an episcopal visitation to the New Mexico part of his vast diocese. Of all the places he visited, none was more interesting than Taos. He recounted his experience with the Comanches at the annual fair and his meeting with Utes. He also told about an Indian raid that occurred after he left:

"In that year, 1760, I left that kingdom at the beginning of July. And on the fourth day of August, according to what they say, nearly three thousand Comanche men waged war with the intention of finishing this pueblo of Taos. They diverted, or provoked, them from a very large house, the greatest in all that valley, belonging to a settler called Villalpando (named Pablo Pando in Domínguez's account), who, luckily for him, had left that day on business. But when they saw so many Comanches coming, many women and men of that settlement took refuge in this house as the strongest. And, trusting in the fact that it had four towers and in the large supply of muskets, powder, and balls, they say that they fired on the Comanches. The latter were infuriated by this to such a horrible degree that they broke into different parts of the house, killed all the men and some women, who also fought. And the wife of the owner of the house, seeing that they were breaking down the outside door, went to defend it with a lance, and she was killed fighting. Fifty-six women and children were carried off, and a large number of horses which the owner of the house was keeping there. Forty-nine bodies of dead Comanches were counted and other trickles of blood were seen."[12]

Through long experience the Spaniards had worked out a sequence of steps for dealing with the Indians: first the peaceful missionary approach, then war if necessary. As a last resort the royal government eventually used bribing as a means of buying off the Indians. The great annual Taos trade fair gave them a chance to pursue the latter method. The fair brought all the tribes—Comanches, Utes, Apaches and occasionally Navajos, friendly and hostile—to Taos to exchange their buffalo hides, buckskins and horses for Spanish goods and Pueblo foodstuffs and to ransom their captives. The Comanches also sold guns, pistols, powder, balls, tobacco, hatchets and vessels made of tin. They obtained these items from other Indians who had direct communication with French traders.[13]

During the fair a universal truce prevailed. Besides the business of trading there was an exchange of captives and a great deal of boisterous revelry. Sometimes the governor came from Santa Fe with his retinue to provide a little order.[14] The fair is described as a brilliant, noisy pageant that lasted day and night and was rivaled only by the trading rendezvous of the mountain men in the nineteenth century. Fray Francisco Atanasio Domínguez, writing in 1776, said "the trading day resembles a second-hand market in Mexico, the way the people mill about."[15] But soon after the fair was over the Comanche and other Indian participants resumed their raiding and plundering.[16]

When Fray Domínguez visited in 1776, he found everyone from the valley, Indian and non-Indian, living in Taos Pueblo where they would stay until the plaza at Ranchos de las Trampas was completed in 1779. It had become apparent to the settlers that they could not continue to live in scattered farm houses and survive the continuing raids by the Comanches, Utes and Apaches. The Comanche raid in 1760 described by Bishop Tamarón was probably a cause for the people banding together to plan and build the plaza.

Because of these raids, Governor Juan Bautista de Anza, as had Governor Pedro Fermin de Mendinueta before him, called attention to the way the new plazas were to be built: two-and three-story houses joined together forming plazas, with portable ladders that could be pulled up in case of attack. He also noted the upper roofs with their embrasures in the parapets for defensive purposes. Domínguez wrote, "This (the plaza at Ranchos de Taos) is being erected by order of the aforesaid governor, Knight [of the Order of Santiago], so that

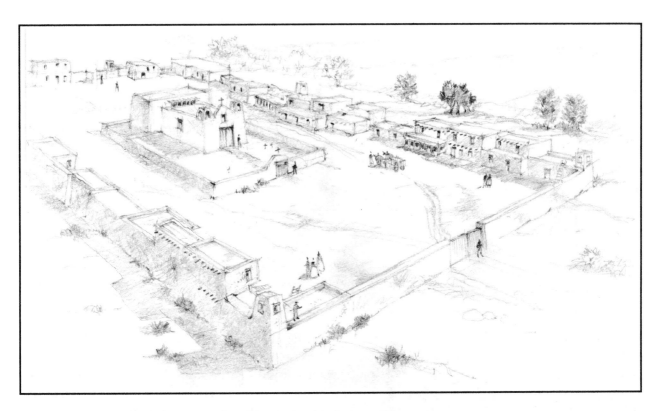

*Illustration 1:1—A sketch of the plaza of Ranchos de Taos as it may have appeared soon after the church of St. Francis of Assisi was completed. Drawn by the author.*

when they live together in this way, even though they are at a distance from the pueblo, they may be able to resist the attack the enemy may make."[17]

The plaza was nearing completion when Fray Juan Agustín de Morfi, in 1788, reported that, "At three leagues (south) from the pueblo is a ranch with abundance of arable lands even more fertile than those of the pueblo...the settlement forms a very spacious quadri-lateral plaza whose houses were almost finished in 1779, with several towers at regular distances for its defense." Neither Domínguez or Morfi said anything about a church in the plaza.[18] Since the present St. Francis of Assisi church was not occupied until 1815, did the largest settlement in the area, outside of the pueblo itself, go without a place to worship for thirty-six years?

The pueblo was three leagues, roughly eight miles away, a good two-hour trip by wagon or carriage, longer through winter snow and over muddy roads after summer downpours. The aged and infirm must have had a hard time getting to San Gerónimo church in the pueblo for services. During the long tenure of Fray José de Vera (1794–1810) the population of Ranchos de Taos grew rapidly, judged by the entries in the baptismal, marriage and burial books in the mission church of San Gerónimo. Father Vera performed all these services in the church at Taos Pueblo. If there was a private chapel somewhere in the Ranchos de Taos area before 1815, no record of it has yet come to light.[19]

In Illustration 1:1 I have tried to show how I and others think the church looked when finished in 1815. Some of this information is gleaned from early documents such as inventories, and some is based on descriptions of how earlier

1:1—Crumbling buildings that formed the exterior wall of the plaza on the northeast side. 1991. Photograph by the author.

1:2—View of the original plaza buildings from the plaza side. 1991. Photograph by the author.

1:3—The high wall is probably part of the two-story building to the right of the church in Photograph 1:7. 1991. Photograph by the author.

churches were built, like those written by Fray Francisco Atanasio Domínguez during his visitation in 1776. Since the church has not been altered too much during its existence, on-site observation has revealed much about how it was built.

The plaza was built in the form of a long rectangle with the long axis running northwest to southeast. It was about eight hundred feet long and four hundred feet wide. There were one-and two-story dwellings located on the perimeter to form the fortress-like exterior walls. Probably, some of these buildings did not abut their neighbors but were connected to the nearest houses by high, thick adobe walls. There were no windows or doors in the exterior walls so all coming and going had to be through two heavy wood gates located in the southeast and northwest plaza walls. The roofs of the buildings were flat, supported by vigas, and constructed in the customary way of the time, as described in Chapter Two. If the builders followed the governor's instructions there were embrasures in the connecting parapet walls which formed battlements between the towers mentioned by Morfi above. The defensive towers were made of adobe and were probably located at the four corners of the plaza, with one or two others in the middle of the long northeast and southwest walls.

The plaza gate, or "puerton," consisted of two leaves that were heavy enough to withstand an armed attack. Each leaf was three and a half to four feet wide and at least eight feet high. Unfortunately no eighteenth-century examples appear to have survived. It is likely these gates turned on pintles as did the church doors, but whether they had a paneled construction or were built up of two layers of wood, as were gates of later date, is not known.[20] Each was no doubt secured with a heavy wooden crossbar on the inside.

The Comanche depredations decreased during the last years of Spanish rule, but harassment by the Utes and Apaches continued. Governor de Anza won a historic victory over the Comanche Chief Cuerno Verde in 1779 and made a treaty with the Comanche tribe that lasted until the occupation by United States troops in 1846. More Spaniards began to settle in Ranchos de Taos and it soon became a typical New Mexican village with the Spanish element dominant in both cultural and economic affairs. The sparsely populated but fertile Taos Valley was now relatively safe for settlers and soon attracted both Spaniards and mixed-bloods from other more crowded places. The village soon extended beyond the walls of the plaza.[21]

During the last decades of the 1700's and early in the 1800's, as the Comanche threat diminished, the settlers once again spread out along the waterways of the valley, but this time instead of building a series of dispersed haciendas they built a defense system with the establishment of several plazas that formed the center of the new villages. By the 1790's several other communities had been established in the valley: the plazas of Nuestra Señora de Guadalupe (Fernando de Taos), La Purisma Concepción (Upper Ranchitos), San Francisco de Paula (Lower Ranchitos), Los Cordovas and Nuestra Señora de los Dolores (Arroyo Hondo). A later example is Nuestra Señora de San Juan de Rio Chiquito (now Talpa) which was established in the early 1800's.[22]

After Governor de Anza made peace with the Comanches he was able to get other tribes to agree to a truce. For some years the lives of the settlers was somewhat peaceful, but never safe from surprise attacks by small bands of Indians who were either unaware of the treaties or did not feel obligated to respect them.

To combat the Apaches, who were still a problem for the settlers, José Maria de Irigoyen, governor of Chihuahua, in the late 1830's established an organization known as La Sociedad Guerra Contra los Barbaros to administer a 100,000-peso bounty fund. He hired James Kirker, an Irish immigrant who became an experienced Indian fighter, to enlist a brigade of privateers. He recruited about a hundred men: hunters, teamsters and pacified Indians. They did not have to wait long for action. Kirker and some fifty of his men were camped near Ranchos de Taos when some Apaches stole some of their horses during the night. The Indians did not know the men were armed for combat, thinking they were

*1:4—This is the rear, or outside wall, of a building on the northeast wall of the plaza. It is a two-story structure with the first floor a few feet below what is now the outside grade. The opening at the bottom was no doubt added later as the original buildings had no openings in the rear wall. This is one of the few remaining parts of the structures that formed the protective walls of the plaza. 1991. Photograph by the author.*

*1:5—A detail of the original roof construction showing how the "rajas," split cedar or other wood, were placed over the vigas and how they rested on the cross beams. 1991. Photograph by the author.*

*1:6—This is an adobe brick from one of the original plaza buildings that was torn down in 1991. It may have been made around 1776. Straw was generously used in the mixture. It measured 18" x 10" x 4". 1991. Photograph by the author.*

traders. As soon as the robbery was discovered Kirker and his men went in pursuit. Kirker knew the Apaches would head for a narrow defile in the nearby mountains. He led his men up the side of the ravine and ambushed the Indians as they rode up on the stolen horses and inflicted heavy losses. The Apaches retreated back toward the village with the idea of seeking refuge in the church. However, they could not get into the church and the plaza proved to be a trap. They lost forty men and all the stolen horses before surrendering. Kirker allowed the survivors to depart, but kept all of the animals in the Indians' possession as booty. The fight, which only lasted about a half-hour, had terrified the villagers who took shelter behind the thick adobe walls and barred doors and windows of their houses and escaped unharmed. Kirker lost only two men.

This account of the "Battle of the Ranch" was written by Matt Field, an unemployed actor turned writer, who was on his way from Missouri to Santa Fe in the summer of 1839. He had stayed several days in Taos and was passing near Ranchos de Taos on his way to Santa Fe the day the fighting occurred. He wrote that the village lay at the base of a gigantic mountain and was watered by a swift stream that rushed from the ravine where the ambush took place. He estimated the village contained about 300 houses which were built compactly together to form a wall enclosing a plaza with the church in the center.[23]

In the early days the plaza was composed entirely of residential buildings and was the center of village life. The construction of the church in 1813–15 provided a strong focal point and village activities soon revolved around it. Saint Francis Day, October 4, continues today as an annual celebration. From the villages of Talpa, Ranchos de Taos, Llano Quemado and Los Cordovas come "Los Comanches," a group of singers and dancers whose performances com-

*1:7—A very early photograph of the Ranchos de Taos plaza looking toward the northeast. The remains of some of these buildings are still standing. Note that the large nave windows had not yet been installed in the church. Courtesy Kit Carson Historic Museums.*

*1:8—A view looking toward the south-west side of the plaza. Store buildings and what may have been a high wall of the Gusdorf mill can be seen. The mill burned in 1895. Courtesy Kit Carson Historic Museums.*

memorate New Year's Day which is chosen to honor Emmanuel, the birth of Christ. Comanche music and dances are performed at the homes where there is someone named Emmanuel, Manuel or Manuelita. On January 25 the Comanches dance at the homes of people named Paul, Pablo or Pablita in honor of St. Paul. Their songs and dances can be traced back to the time their ancestors were prisoners of various Indian tribes including the Comanches.[24]

During the early years of the nineteenth century changes were taking place in the religious life of the settlers. The church was no longer being subsidized by royal decree. The clergy was more dependent on fees and support from the more affluent of the parishioners. Tension was building up between the secular priests

*1:9—A procession is moving out of the churchyard in this photograph made sometime between 1915 and 1920. The date on the cross is March, 1915, but that date remained in place for several years. Courtesy Kit Carson Historic Museums.*

and the Franciscan missionaries. In 1813 the Spanish "cortes," parliament, ordered secularization. When Mexico declared its independence from Spain in 1821 the Spanish friars were driven out of the country. According to some Catholic historians, when the Franciscans were asked to leave their missions, some of them chose to stay. It has been disputed that this was the only reason for the decline of the Franciscan ministry.

Spain's hold on its colonies began to slip in the early 1800's as a spirit of independence swept the New World. Mexico declared its freedom from Spain in August, 1821, but because of the isolation of New Mexico word did not reach Santa Fe for several weeks. As soon as it did, officials announced an end to the restrictive trade policies Spain had imposed and welcomed the American traders who were coming in from the east. Soon the Santa Fe Trail was carrying wagon loads of goods from Missouri to be sold at great profit to New Mexicans. However, the Mexican government began imposing its own set of rules and taxes on the traders. Civil strife created fear among the populace and there was real concern over what might happen following the successful Texas war for independence from Mexico in 1836.

There was mounting pressure in the United States to acquire the Southwest, New Mexico to California, as part of the doctrine of Manifest Destiny. An offer to purchase the land was turned down by Mexico and tension increased when Texas was annexed by the United States in 1845. Mexico had never recognized the independence of Texas and sent an invading army across the lower Rio Grande which engaged in battle with American troops on land claimed by the United States. President James K. Polk used this as a reason to announce a state of war with Mexico. Colonel Stephen Watts Kearny was placed in command of an army to take control of the Southwest.

Kearny organized his troops in Missouri and in June, 1846, struck out on the Santa Fe Trail for New Mexico with 1600 men, artillery and supply wagons. He met no organized resistance and arrived in Santa Fe on August 18. Kearny spent some time establishing a governance for the territory which included the appointment of Charles Bent of Taos as governor. Kearny, now a general, left a small contingent of troops in Santa Fe under the command of Colonel Sterling Price and headed for California. A plan was conceived in northern New Mexico to rebel against the American occupation and in January, 1847, Bent and several others were killed in and around Taos. Price marched with a contingent of 353 men from Santa Fe through deep snow, past encounters at Embudo and Santa Cruz, to find the rebels inside the church at Taos Pueblo. A fierce bombardment followed which destroyed the church. Some of the remains still stand. The rebel surrender ended the resistance to the American occupation.[26]

After the United States occupation of New Mexico and the abortive Taos Rebellion of January, 1847, troops were stationed in the Taos Valley to protect against Apache and Ute raids and to discourage further dissent by the pueblo and settlers. They were first garrisoned in the village of Taos and later at Canton-

*1:10—Alex Gusdorf built this steam-powered flour mill on the southwest side of the plaza in 1879. Unfortunately, it burned to the ground in 1895 and he moved his business to Taos, dealing a heavy blow to the economy of Ranchos de Taos. Courtesy Kit Carson Historic Museums.*

ment Burgwin, built in 1852, six miles south of Ranchos de Taos, on the Rito de la Olla. The garrison was named for Captain John Burgwin, who was killed at the pueblo during the rebellion.[27] Supplying provisions for the men and horses helped the cash-short farmers of the valley. Naturally prices went up and corn, wheat and fodder became more difficult to secure. Lt. J.H. Whittlesey, who blamed high flour prices on the large amounts of wheat used to make whiskey, wrote "...of the most deleterious nature" (of the famous Taos Lightning), and hoped legislation would be enacted "...to stop the pernicious traffic."[28]

The change in the government also brought a great change in the church. On July 19, 1850, Pope Pius IX established by decree the vicariate apostolic of New Mexico and on the 23rd of that month he named Jean Baptiste Lamy as vicar apostolic. Bishop Lamy arrived in Santa Fe in 1851 and immediately tried to gain control of the church and its missions. This led to conflict with Padre José Martinez who was the priest at Our Lady of Guadalupe Church in Don Fernando de Taos. Lamy eventually replaced Martinez with Father Damasio Taladrid, a secular priest from Spain.[29]

During the nineteenth century wheat production and the milling of flour were the life-blood of the Ranchos de Taos economy. In 1871, Alexander Gusdorf, immigrant to New Mexico from Germany, moved from Peñasco to the village to manage a mill and general merchandise store owned by his uncle Zadoc Staab, an affluent Santa Fe merchant. Gusdorf quickly established himself as a community leader and is credited with introducing threshing machines and self-tying binders to the valley as well as planting the first fruit orchard there. In 1879 he

*1:11—The interior of the Tomás Rivera store on the southwest side of the plaza opposite the church sometime in the 1920's. Shown in the photograph are Rivera, Eva Rivera Martinez and an unidentified woman. Courtesy of Eva Rivera Martinez.*

bought out his uncle and constructed a three-story steam-powered flour mill, the first of its kind in New Mexico. It was located on the southwest side of the Ranchos plaza just south of the church. The mill burned to the ground in 1895, a serious blow to the village economy, and Gusdorf moved his headquarters to Don Fernando de Taos.[30] Gusdorf later became the president and chairman of the board of the First State Bank of Taos. When he died in 1923 he was succeeded by his German-born wife, Bertis (Bertha).[31]

Other businesses were located around the plaza at different times. In the early 1900's Tomás Rivera had a general merchandise store on the southwest side opposite the church and he and his family lived in the house next door. From a photograph of the interior of the store it appears that he did in fact carry almost anything a family could need: foodstuff, cloth, clothing, farm tools and many other items. According to his daughter, Eva Rivera Martinez, who still lives in the family home on the plaza, Tomás Rivera owned the first automobile in Ranchos de Taos.[32]

Today, on the northwest side of the plaza, there is a group of buildings that is now separated from it by the highway. In the 1890's this area was occupied by the residence and general store of "Squire" Hart.[33] They were later owned by the Martinez family. Today the Ranchos de Taos post office, the old motion picture theater and some stores are located there. The motion picture theater has not operated for several years. Martinez Hall, the two-story building with the three windows in front, was the scene of many Saturday night dances and is still used for receptions and other gatherings. It was a hangout for many of the more famous Taos artists and they did paintings on the walls of the ballroom, some of which are still there today.

Behind the post office and the stores there is an area called "Plaza Vieja" (the old plaza) by local people, among whom are Eva Martinez and Talpa resident Manuel Morgas. There is an open space with some houses around it and remains of a stone wall on the northwest side. A spring, which is still active next to the present highway, provided a good supply of water and may have been the reason for the location of the houses. It is possible that as the main plaza became filled to capacity an extension was made to the northwest side. But since it is called Plaza Vieja, it must be older than the main plaza. Perhaps houses were built by the early settlers before the Ranchos plaza was constructed. I have found no written description of Plaza Vieja, but the older residents all know it as such.[34]

Village life did not change much during the twenties and early thirties. On April 22, 1937, St. Francis of Assisi Church was made a parish, 122 years after the first pastor, José Benito Pereyro, was assigned to minister to the parish as an "ayuda," or visita, of San Gerónimo parish at Taos Pueblo. Reverend José A. Garcia was appointed the first pastor of the new parish. He was born in 1904, attended St. Francis and St. Michael's schools in Santa Fe, and took his seminary training at St. Patrick's Seminary in Menlo, California. He was ordained a priest by Archbishop Daeger in Santa Fe on June 29, 1929. Garcia served at Ranchos de Taos until 1944 when he was made Vicar General by Archbishop

*1:12—From the vintage of the automobile it would seem that this picture was made sometime around 1920. This may have been the automobile owned by Tomás Rivera, the first one in Ranchos de Taos. Avery Collection, New Mexico State Records Center and Archives. Negative 9331.*

*1:13—Northwest side of the plaza January, 1943, seen over the buttress of the church. Photograph by John Collier. Office of War Information Collection, Prints and Photographic Division, Library of Congress. LC-USW 3-13735C.*

Byrne. Later he was appointed a domestic prelate with the title of Rt. Rev. Monsignor by Pope Pius XXII and in 1957 he was given the title of Protonotary Apostolic. Garcia was one of the most distinguished priests in the Southwest.[35]

Garcia had not been at St. Francis long before he began planning to build a parish house. He wrote Archbishop R. E. Gerken on June 1, 1937, that he was in the process of acquiring land for the new building and was going to have the parishioners make the adobes. He sent the Archbishop a copy of the plan for the house and after some correspondence back and forth Gerken approved it. Work proceeded slowly, but it was finished early the next year. It is located across the street on the northeast side of the church.[36]

On April 17, 1939, Father Garcia wrote Archbishop Gerken that he had heard that the highway from Santa Fe to Taos, which was being planned, would avoid Ranchos de Taos and go to the northwest through Cordillera because of a local squabble over two routes proposed by the State Highway Department. The Department had surveyed one route that would take the new road through the Ranchos de Taos plaza just southeast of the church; the other would be where it was finally placed, northwest of the church. Garcia said that he had not taken sides on the issue, although importuned by both parties. He was more concerned that if the road did not go through the Ranchos de Taos plaza the church would lose money from the tourists, the people would be greatly inconvenienced and the visitors would miss the most interesting sights on the road to Taos.[37]

*1:14—The plaza, January, 1943. Photograph by John Collier, Office of War Information Collection, Prints and Photographic Division, Library of Congress. LC-USW 3-13728C.*

*1:15—This photograph is titled "Village scene at noon, Ranchos de Taos." Photograph by Arthur Rothstein, April, 1936, Farm Security Administration Collection, Prints and Photographic Division, Library of Congress. LC USW 3-16950.*

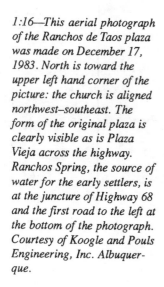

*1:16—This aerial photograph of the Ranchos de Taos plaza was made on December 17, 1983. North is toward the upper left hand corner of the picture: the church is aligned northwest–southeast. The form of the original plaza is clearly visible as is Plaza Vieja across the highway. Ranchos Spring, the source of water for the early settlers, is at the juncture of Highway 68 and the first road to the left at the bottom of the photograph. Courtesy of Koogle and Pouls Engineering, Inc. Albuquerque.*

Other citizens of the Taos area were not as noncommittal as Father Garcia and strongly challenged the routing of the road to the south across the front of Saint Francis Church. On July 6 the Taos Artists Association, composed of forty-six members, sent a telegram to the Archbishop asking him to intercede with Governor Miles "...to prevent the immediate destruction of the Ranchos de Taos plaza by the contemplated routing of the Santa Fe–Taos highway." The telegram continued, "The beauty, historic value and actual use of the church will be virtually ruined should this road pass directly in front of it. Stop." They indicated that this routing was proposed by a single person interested in improving his business. They also pointed out the responsibility of the Catholic church to stop such "vandalism." They felt the road would endanger people entering and leaving the church.[38]

Some Taos citizens, mostly from the artists' community, formed the "Save the Ranchos Plaza Committee" and began a campaign to put the highway to the north of the church where the road was then located. The road to Santa Fe at that time ran about a third of a mile southeast of the present state highway parallel to it. It reached the plaza at the southwest corner, turned left and went behind the buildings that form the southwest wall of the plaza, from which it turned northeast in front of the buildings that form the northwest side of the plaza.

Archbishop Gerken contacted Governor John Miles and according to the newspaper account placed before him the protests from the artists' association.

Miles said the decision was up to the Taos County Commission. He said, "Personally I'm not favoring one route or the other." Highway Engineer Burton G. Dwyre said, "The Highway Department desires to do what the people want. It is not insistent upon any given location, in front or in back of the church, provided it is one that the Bureau of Public Roads will approve. It must be remembered it will pay two-thirds of the cost."[39] The Governor replied to Gerken with a letter reiterating what he had said when they met.[40]

Local residents tell the story that Eleanor Roosevelt, Frances Perkins, Secretary of the Interior, Mabel Dodge Luhan and others were asked to use their influence to have the road located north of the church and they did indeed intervene through contacts with the state officials.[41] According to a statement made by Dorothy Benrimo to Tonie Haegler in the early sixties, Barbara Latham Cook, of Talpa, wrote a letter to Mrs. Roosevelt who then sent an aide to review the situation. It is assumed that after the aide reported back to her she contacted the officials and used her influence to change the routing of the highway.[42]

Ben F. Harbert, secretary of the Taos Chamber of Commerce, sent Archbishop Gerken a copy of a resolution from the Chamber on July 14 which said in part, "The action (the resolution) of the Chamber of Commerce only reflects the general sentiment of the whole Taos Valley touching the location of the highway through the Plaza of Ranchos."[43]

On the fifteenth *The New Mexican*, a Santa Fe newspaper, ran a letter from Mrs. Andrew Dasburg which said she had sent copies of the petition to all parties involved including the Bureau of Public Roads in Denver.[44] On the eighteenth, in the "Capitol" column in *The New Mexican*, Dwyre was quoted as saying that the Bureau of Public Roads preferred the route north of the church. He said it would be surveyed and if workable the Highway Department would recommend it to the County Commission.[45]

*The El Taoseño* newspaper came out with a headline on November 15, 1939, reading "Road Crew Moves In to Start on Ranchos Road." The sub-head said, "Brown Brothers of Albuquerque Locate Camp South of Town to Start on Bridge Structures." The story told that Brown had been the low bidder on the four miles of highway from Taos to Ranchos de Taos, having bid a little over $128,000. This was the beginning of the construction that would replace the old road and link Santa Fe to Taos with a new paved highway located, at least in Ranchos de Taos, where the people wanted it. [46] So the highway was built across the northwest part of the plaza where the old road was located, but as it left the plaza heading southwest it followed a new route north of the old road, the route it follows today. The documents in the Archives of the Archdiocese do not say who made the final decision on routing, but it must have been the County Commission following the recommendations of the Highway Department and the Bureau of Public Roads. Obviously the Archbishop's influence and the sentiments of the people of the Taos Valley, and maybe even Mrs. Roosevelt, had a strong impact on the decision makers. This threat to the integrity of the plaza

*1:17—Northwest side of the plaza in 1991. Photograph by the author.*

*1:18—Northwest side of the plaza in 1991. Photograph by the author.*

*1:19—The tavern which has stood on the southern corner of the plaza for many years is still in operation. Photograph by the author, 1991.*

brought forth an unprecedented out-pouring of feeling for the plaza and the church. The artists and the business people realized the importance of the plaza and church to the whole Taos Valley and wanted to protect them from the degradation they felt the highway alignment to the south of the church would cause. Not until 1967 when the church was threatened with the application of cement stucco instead of mud plaster was there another citizen movement to protect it.

During the last thirty or so years tourism has become a much more important source of income to the Taos economy and the desire to visit the church greatly increased. Fewer people live on the plaza now. There are many shops and boutiques that cater to the tourist trade including a shop on the northeast side next to the rectory operated by the church that is part of one of the original plaza buildings. The tavern still sits in the southwest corner and the site to the north of it, where Alexander Gusdorf's Great Western flour mill was located, is now a part of Eva Rivera Martinez's yard. The ruins of some of the original buildings lie neglected on the northeast wall of the old plaza and there is a sign on the building that was once the local pool hall that says, "Will Build to Suit," so they are endangered. In the summer of 1991 part of one of the surviving ruins was torn down and the vigas and some original adobes were salvaged. I am afraid it will not be long before all that now remains of the original buildings forming the plaza will be gone. In September, 1994, I observed that more deterioration had occurred and what walls remained were covered with graffiti.

Automobile traffic on the Santa Fe highway has increased enormously in the last several years, creating a greater physical separation of the buildings on the northwest side of the plaza from the rest of it. On any given day during the tourist season the plaza area northwest of the church is filled with parked cars, as is the area in front of the entrance to the church yard on the southeast. At times there are two or three large buses parked in front of the church with their motors running, filling the air with noise and fumes while their passengers visit the church. The streets around the church have been crudely paved and have many speed bumps to slow down the automobile traffic. As the interest in St. Francis of Assisi Church has increased, taking care of the tourist traffic, particularly the parking, has become a severe problem which must be dealt with or the visual aspect of the church will suffer.

I have not found any record of archaeological studies made in or around the church or plaza. It would have been an excellent time to do some archaeological work in the church before the concrete floor was installed around 1960, or when the extensive repairs were done in 1966–67. George Wright, the architect for the latter work, lamented that this was not done because of the time constraints.[47] Before it is too late a study should be made of the church and the buildings forming the plaza that are still in use and those now in ruin to see what can be learned about what life was like in the plaza many years ago.

*1:20—The abandoned pool hall on the northeast side of the plaza is likely to be torn down soon. Photograph by the author. December, 1991.*

## *CHAPTER 2—H0W ST. FRANCIS OF ASSISI CHURCH WAS BUILT*

B ased on newly found photographs, documents and other information, and on what can be seen in other older churches, we can determine when and how the Spanish settlers of Ranchos de las Trampas built their church. Until quite recently there has been much conjecture and indecision about the time of the building of the church at Ranchos de Taos (which is named in Spanish San Francisco de Asís, or in English, Saint Francis of Assisi). The writer-historian John Kessell states that documents in the Archives of the Archdiocese of Santa Fe firmly establish the date of the licensing as 1813 and probable completion of the church as 1815.[1]

Through the years it was anybody's guess when the church was actually built and everyone formed their own opinion. George Kubler states in *Religious Architecture of New Mexico*, written in 1939–1940 after an intensive study of the mission church, that there is no reliable evidence of the date of construction. Tree-ring studies indicated 1816 plus or minus ten years as the age of the vigas (roof timbers).[2] Governor L. Bradford Prince in *Spanish Mission Churches of New Mexico* gives the date of construction as 1779.[3] In a pamphlet, author unknown, which used to be sold to visitors at the church it is asserted that the plans for the church were drawn in Spain and that construction began in 1710 and took forty-five years to complete.[4]

In the summer of 1810, forty-two-year-old Fray José Benito Pereyro, superior of the Franciscans of New Mexico, moved from Santa Clara Pueblo to San Gerónimo de Taos church in Taos Pueblo. A Spaniard from the province of Galicía, he had already served in New Mexico for sixteen years. As missionary pastor of San Gerónimo he had spiritual responsibility for all the inhabitants of the pueblo, Spanish settlers and "people of all classes" living in the area, including the families living down in the valley three leagues southwest at Ranchos de Taos in the plaza of San Francisco de las Trampas.[5]

After he stepped down as the superior in the spring of 1812, the people living in and around the Ranchos de Taos plaza discussed with Pereyro the need for their own church and the license they would have to obtain in order to build it. Evidently in response to a query from them, the diocesan office in Durango, Mexico, decreed the procedure the people of Ranchos de Taos should follow in acquiring the license. The decree is dated August 4, 1812. It said the people must document the need for the church and get certification of the local authorities.[6]

The successor to Pereyro as superior, Fray Antonio Caballero, replied on September 22, 1812, that a chapel at the Plaza of San Francisco would be most convenient and that the settlement was large enough to maintain it properly. That same day the alcalde mayor, or district officer of Taos, endorsed the request, but the governor, José Manrique, did not respond until March 20, 1813. Final approval from the diocese of Durango was dated September 20, 1813. The approval stated that "...said citizens are responsible for providing whatever repairs it may require for its preservation, and for maintaining it in cleanliness...." The parishioners of today are still living up to the responsibilities stated in the old document.

Kessell surmises that because of the distance between Taos and Durango, some eleven hundred miles, the license probably didn't reach the citizens of San Francisco de las Trampas until the weather was too cold to start building. He assumes that construction began in the spring of 1814 and continued until the cold weather shut down the exterior work. Interior finishing might have continued during the winter. The church was nearing completion in the summer of 1815. On July 13, 1815, Ignacio Durán sent a formal petition to the provincial "custos," or superior of the Franciscans, Fray Isidoro Barcenilla, on behalf of himself and his neighbors, asking for the services of Fray José Benito Pereyro in the plazas of San Francisco de las Trampas and of San Francisco de Paula (Lower Ranchitos) for which services he would be paid with grain, the custom in those days. The well-off would give two "fanegas," and the poor, one "fanega," which is 1.58 bushels.

Permission was granted by Fray Barcenilla and Fray Pereyro became the pastor. The church, or chapel, was consecrated, for he wrote to Durango sometime in the fall asking permission to bury inside the new chapel. It was called a "capilla," a chapel, not because of its size, but because of its dependency, as a "visita" of the mission church of San Gerónimo de Taos. The reply giving approval was signed in Durango on January 9, 1816. An 1818 note added to the earliest known inventory of the church, dated October 29, 1817, proclaimed, "This temple was constructed at the expense of the Reverend Father Minister Fray José Benito Pereyro and the citizenry of the Plaza." Unfortunately Pereyro did not record the date the church was dedicated. It may have been in the fall of 1815. He was later severely criticized for his poor record keeping, among other things.[7]

There is some question whether the church could have been built in the time from the receipt of the approval until the first services were held in the summer of 1815. Perhaps the settlers had started work before getting the formal authorization to proceed.

The Franciscan priests usually drew the plans for the churches and since Fray Pereyro was credited with possibly being an artist, a "santero," and one of the ones who financed the construction, he probably did design it. Fray Pereyro brought to St. Francis of Assisi church a refinement of architectural design and detail not found in most of the earlier New Mexico churches. He had been influenced by the churches he was familiar with in Spain and he had visited and served in several churches in Mexico and this area. The original church design was certainly in good proportion and good taste, showing he had learned the subtleties of layout that enhanced the religious feeling in churches.

Since the plaza had been built over three decades before the church, the site and size of the church were pretty well established. It was laid out on the long axis of the plaza facing southeast toward the main plaza entrance. The Franciscans in New Mexico did not follow any set rule as to which direction their churches should face but many were oriented east or south to catch the sunlight during morning services. The floor plan of Saint Francis is a little different from the earlier churches in that the wings of the transept, at about thirteen feet, are deeper than most others. Kubler wrote, "...the transepts constitute a separate church at right angles to the nave: the north (northeast) arm contains an altar in a kind of sanctuary formed with steps and other furniture. The south (southwest) arm is deep enough to serve as a nave for this church within a church."[8] The Saint Joseph altar and screen painted by Molleno were located here. They have long since disappeared. They may be in collections of the Denver Art Museum or they may have been purchased by an individual.[9]

Kubler observed that in most early New Mexico churches the walls of the nave were not parallel but sloped inward from the rear of the nave toward the altar. In the case of this church the walls of the nave are essentially parallel, sloping toward the crossing only a couple of inches from front to rear of the nave. However, the walls of the transept are not square with the walls of the nave, being off by as much five degrees which, when looked at in plan, tilts the axis to the right. The rear wall of the sanctuary and the altar follow the alignment of the northwest walls of the transept. Kubler notes that some medieval churches in Europe frequently show a similar multiplicity of axes, and according to legend this irregularity symbolizes the drooping of the head of Christ on the cross. However, he found that this deviation of axes also occurred in continuous nave churches where the plan does not symbolize the cross.

Kubler noted other things in the design of St. Francis such as adherence to the conventional proportions of the nave where the height is about the same as the width, the width being set sometimes by the length of available vigas.[10] Here the height at the crossing is approximately 22'-0" to the bottom of the ceiling boards and the width is 22'-10". The same vertical measurement at the face of the choir loft is 22'-4" and the width is approximately 25'-0", so there is a slight slope of the ceiling toward the crossing. The wood floor that was in place in 1934, when the measurements were taken, sloped about seven to eight inches from the rear wall of the nave to the center of the crossing.[11]

One of the strongest design elements built into the church by Fray Pereyro was the clerestory window which brought light onto the main altar. Kubler believed that the clerestory window was a New Mexico invention since the church builders in this area did not erect domes over the crossing as was common in colonial churches in Mexico and other parts of this country. He felt that the small irregularities we have mentioned coupled with the dramatic clerestory lighting are sufficient to focus all attention on the sanctuary. He noted that the small nave windows in most churches added little light and the nave, in effect, acts as a dark tunnel. Kubler said, "The eye is unable to resist the directional force of this contrasted system of lighting: the attention is immediately drawn, as in a theater, to the sanctuary."[12] This would have been true in the Ranchos de Taos church when it was first built since the windows in the nave were small and high. Lt. J. W. Abert attended a Mass at noon in the "parroquia" of Santa Fe in 1846 and described the light on the altar: "From a high window a flood of crimson light, tinged by the curtain as it passed through, poured down upon the altar." The light could only have come from a clerestory window.[13] There were 28 panes in the clerestory window at St. Francis before it was remodeled in 1967.

When Fray Domínguez made the census in 1776 he counted 67 families with 306 persons from Trampas de Taos who were then living in the pueblo or on scattered ranches while the plaza was being built.[14] There were enough people living in the valley and available to build the church thirty or so years after the Comanche raids had stopped.

It is interesting to note that some of the materials and methods of building introduced by the Spanish in 1610 were still in use when construction began on St. Francis of Assisi some two hundred years later.

The method of making adobes in the early 1800's was no doubt little different than that used today when the adobe maker has no mechanical equipment to help him. The material for making adobes is abundant and easily collected in the Taos Valley. The clay–sand mixture mixed with water is kneaded with a hoe, or maybe bare feet, into an even paste. Straw is worked in, supposedly to act as a binder to prevent cracking during curing and to add strength, but its value is questionable. However, when used in adobe plaster straw adds a certain texture which is undeniably beautiful especially when it catches the late-afternoon sun. Today the mud and straw mixture is poured into wooden gang forms of a dozen or more molds and allowed to dry for two or three days on the ground. The bricks have by then shrunk away from the sides of the mold and are removed and stacked on edge to dry for two weeks or longer depending on the weather. The Spanish settlers introduced the use of wood forms into New Mexico in the seventeenth century.[15] In the early days long lengths of boards were hard to come by so the forms were only made to hold one or two bricks at a time. That would have slowed down the process. The adobe making season in the Taos Valley usually extends from late March through September and normally has a frost-free period of about 120 days. It is doubtful that frost-protection measures were available in 1813–1814. Still it is possible that the parishioners made enough adobe bricks within the time frame.

The size of the adobes used in the early churches varied quite a bit. An adobe brick saved when the church was being restored in 1967 is now on display in the parish hall. It measures 14 by 10 by 4 inches and is smaller than other bricks that have been measured. Adobe bricks found in San Miguel Church in Santa Fe, rebuilt in 1710, were about 20 by 12 by 4 inches.[16] Kubler says the average brick used in Spanish colonial times was 18 by 10 by 5 inches and weighed fifty or sixty pounds. It usually represented the load which one man could handle.[17] The adobes in the ruins of the buildings which formed the plaza of Ranchos de Trampas, in 1776, measure 18 by 11 by 4 inches.

I have estimated that around 85,000 adobe bricks of the size made then would be needed to build the church (without the buttresses and sacristy which were probably added later). It also has been estimated that two men using nothing but hoes and shovels and wood forms can make about 300 bricks in a long summer day.[18] So it would have taken eight men about seventy working days to make the 85,000 bricks for the church; sixteen men could have done it in half that time, less than two months, assuming they could take time off from their farms and livestock.

In those days there were several ways to build a foundation. One method was to dig a trench a foot or two deep and fill it with stones, generally rounded river rock, and pour mud around them to fill the excavation. Another was to lay a few courses of adobe brick from the bottom of the trench to grade, assuming that the adobes were harder and more resistive to water damage than the earth that was removed. A method which may have been used at St. Francis church was to smooth and tamp the earth and build directly upon it. No excavations were made to determine the footings under the main walls of the church when recent restoration projects were done. When the buttresses had to be removed and rebuilt in 1979 no foundations were found, but a layer of ashes and charcoal several inches thick was beneath them. Kubler wrote that in some of the mission churches built in the 1600's ashes were placed under the walls: "...the fire producing the charred wood was part of the process of construction. It is well known that charcoal is an efflorescent substance, repelling water, and its use in foundations is a process of very great antiquity, intended to protect the structure from moisture at building level."[19]

The exterior walls were built fairly straight vertically. They extended a foot or two above the roof to form a parapet. Based on what was seen in 1967 when the old plaster was removed, the high nave walls may have been built as cavity walls, with a space separating the inner and outer walls. This can be seen in Photograph 3:3. No thorough investigation of this wall construction was made in 1967, but the walls were reinforced to prevent further separation.

In order to accommodate the clerestory windows the walls of the transept at Ranchos de Taos were brought up about five feet higher than the nave walls as were the walls around the sanctuary. The viga and corbel ends protruded through the southeast-facing wall only above the clerestory windows, not at the transepts.

During the time the adobes were being made, cured and laid in the walls, pine and fir trees were cut and the logs brought down from the mountains. There were some thirty vigas 32 feet or more long used over the nave, twenty-eight in the transept 25 feet long, and eleven above the sanctuary of varying length. Timbers were also needed to support the choir loft and to make columns, corbels, lintels and other items. Trees used in this manner are usually cut in the fall of the year before the snow falls, or in the spring before the ground thaws and the mud gets too deep. Once they were pulled from the mountain forests to the site of the church by teams of oxen, the logs were peeled of their bark with draw knives or hand adzes. The timbers used for corbels, lintels and other squared members were laboriously cut with hand saws and then crudely carved as is shown in the HABS rubbings and drawings.

The vigas cured on the ground while the walls were being erected and then were set in place, but how was that done? Unfortunately construction methods were seldom described in writing in early days but were passed from generation to generation. Today all we can do is surmise about how some feats were accomplished. Each 32-foot log would have weighed between 600 and 700 pounds, so it would require several men to raise it to the top of the wall and set it across the space it was to span if they were using only ropes as shown in Illustration 2:2.

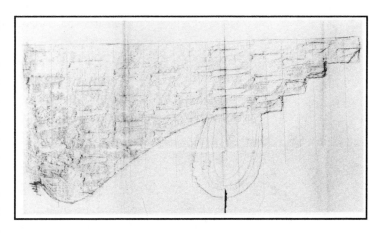

*Illustration 2:1—A rubbing of an old corbel made by the Historic American Building Survey (HABS) in 1934, Prints and Photographic Division, Library of Congress.*

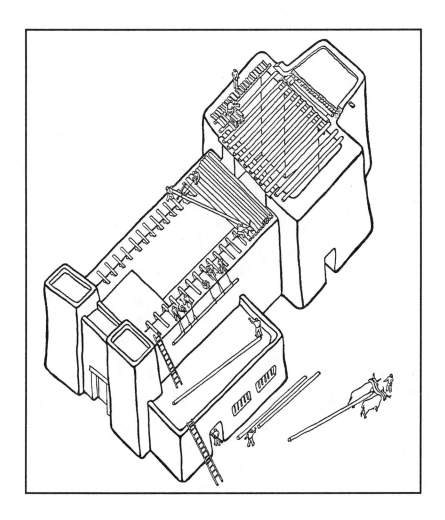

*Illustration 2:2—Hypothetical view of roof-construction process in the seventeenth century. Drawn by Elizabeth Kubler. From* Religious Architecture of New Mexico, *University of New Mexico Press.*

This drawing, Illustration 2:2, shows the whole roof-building process as George Kubler envisioned it. Six men standing on top of the thick nave walls are lifting a viga with ropes. Each man would be lifting about 125 pounds which is easily done by the average construction worker. Once to the top it is walked around to its final location. Three men are moving a viga into position while others are laying the ceiling boards over other vigas. Kubler wrote, "We do not know how the roof timbers were maneuvered into position, once the walls had been brought to the required height. The problem may bear upon the phenomenon of the thicker wall. Whatever the method, a fulcrum at some point above the intended roof level was needed. That hoisting cranes were contrived for this purpose seems unlikely. The time and labor expended in setting up a hoisting yard and in fashioning adequate pulley blocks would have been out of proportion both to the amount of work required from the crane and to the amount of work involved in the routine process of building more wall. A large number of men posted at roof level perhaps provided the fulcrum, but only one wall of platform-like thickness would have been needed to accommodate them."[20]

Other historians disagree with Kubler and believe pulleys were used in one form or another. Pulleys were in use in the Middle East at least fifteen hundred years B.C. primarily to raise water from wells. The Greeks and Romans perfected them and created multiple sets of pulley-blocks to raise huge stones.[21] The Spanish used pulleys on their ships as well as in construction so the settlers knew about them, and almost every farmer had pulleys as prized implements. James Ivey, an archaeologist-historian, writing for the National Park Service, says shear legs were used to hoist roof beams on New Mexico churches as early as the construction of the Salinas Missions in the early seventeenth century. He

*Illustration 2:3—A lithograph by Joseph Imhof, probably done in the 1940's or 1950's, in which the artist presents his concept of how St. Francis of Assisi Church was built. The priest in the foreground is, no doubt, Fray José Benito Pereyro directing the construction. Imhof does not show the sacristy or buttresses in place so he must have assumed they were not part of the original construction. An original print of this lithograph is in the possession of the Maxwell Museum, the University of New Mexico. St. Francis of Assisi Church Archives.*

*2:1—An old photograph showing Taos Indians raising a pole or viga. St. Francis of Assisi Church Archives.*

describes shear-legs as a simple lifting device made by two spars fastened together at the top, set on the ground and several feet taller than the top of the wall, from which a pulley system was hung. Ground crews using guy-ropes controlled the tilt of the legs.[22]

The Taos artist, Joseph Imhof, made a lithograph showing how he thought the church was constructed. He conjectured that the builders used a simple rope hoist sitting on top of the wall to lift the vigas into place. Imhof showed all the workers to be Indians which was not the case. The inhabitants of the plaza may have hired some Indians from the pueblo to help, but not to do all the work

It would have been possible, although difficult, to set up a hoisting operation as drawn by Imhof, or a shear-legs device as described by Ivey to raise the vigas to roof level.

Another method of raising vigas to roof height is shown in Photograph 2:1. The Indians are using several long poles lashed together to form an "x" to lift a long viga. Once the end of the viga is at roof level, it could be pulled into position with ropes.

Usually the vigas were placed on top of the corbels with the smaller diameter ends set in the direction the roof was supposed to drain. In the case of St. Francis Church the roof of the nave and sanctuary were made to drain in both directions by the sloping of the earth fill. Only the roof over the transept sloped in one direction: toward the southeast. Over the vigas, split lengths of wood, usually cedar, called "rajas," were placed, or "latillas" which were peeled aspen, cottonwood or juniper poles were used. Latillas were usually laid in a herringbone pattern on top of the vigas. The rajas used over the buildings now in ruin, which were part of the original plaza construction, are very roughly split boards and are about thirty to thirty-six inches long and about four inches wide. Grass, reeds or other vegetal material was placed over the latillas or rajas. In the old plaza buildings there is no evidence of any such material having been laid over the rajas under the considerable earth fill, as much as sixteen inches in places. Usually several inches of tamped earth were laid with a slope toward the drainage points. The earth was topped with a hard troweled coat of adobe plaster which provided some protection against leaking. When the inevitable leaks did occur and were located, they were repaired simply by adding more dirt and packing it down. In time the earth on top of the vigas could easily reach a depth that threatened the bearing capacity of the roof structure. The parishioners, no doubt, spent a great deal of time through the years keeping the church roof repaired. Most of the roof leaks occurred around the canales. The run-off from them would fall, or be blown, against the wall below, eroding the mud plaster and adobe brick.[23]

The dirt fill on the roof continually sifted through the ceiling and was a great annoyance to the worshipers below. The church had to be constantly cleaned. When inexpensive cloth became available the women of the church tacked long strips of the material sewn together, usually white muslin, "techos,"under the vigas running from wall to wall over the choir loft only. Then narrow strips of the cloth, dipped in a flour-water mixture were used to cover the joints along the bottom of the vigas. The "techos" protected the choir members from the falling dirt. A piece of this cloth can be seen hanging below the vigas in Photograph 2:4 made in 1934. The cloth was taken down, washed and rehung each year before the Feast of St. Francis.[24] The height of the vigas above the nave and the rest of the church precluded the hanging of cloth there.

When Fray Domínguez visited Santa Fe in 1776 he described the floors in the parish church of St. Francis as "...bare earth packed down like mud. This is the usual floor throughout these regions."  There were exceptions such San Gerónimo at Taos Pueblo, the floor of which he said was all covered with beams from front to back. He must have been referring to "vigas labradas," wrought beams, which can mean any treatment of the rough timber to make it more suitable for its purpose, from dressing, hewing or squaring it, to carving it.[25] The earthen floors were sometimes covered with a thin mixture of clay and animal blood.[26]

Fray Domínquez also gave a detailed account of the exterior appearance of the churches he inventoried in 1776. In all likelihood St. Francis Church in Ranchos de Taos was similar to those he visited that were north of Santa Fe. There were usually a pair of wide doors, squared, not arched, with two or more panels in each, some with a wicket in one of them.[27] We know from the early records that the doors at St. Francis were donated and that they were carved. The HABS surveyors found the pivot holes in the old lintel where the pintle was held and noted that in Section "C" on Sheet 26 of their drawings. This indicates that the doors were approximately thirteen feet high and four feet wide, large enough to drive animals and wagons through in case of attack.[28] Most church doors were secured in those days by a crossbar. However, Gustavo Fernandez said that he found a large metal key, eight to ten inches long, in the bottom pivot hole which had been hollowed out of a rock. He still has the key which he thinks was the key to the front doors. Fernandez was a cabinet maker and carpenter who worked on the church at many different times. He made the new front doors installed in 1967, and the pews and other furniture in the church. He also served on the parish council and was president at one time.[29]

Because the church was built like a fortress the windows were small and set high in the nave walls. There was no set pattern for location of windows in New Mexico churches. Some churches had two windows on only one side of the nave, some had windows at the end of the transept, and others had windows located as at St. Francis. There was usually a window at the rear of the choir loft over the main entrance. There is uncertainty about the glazing material used in these and the clerestory windows. It was not until the 1850's that window glass began to be imported from the United States. An observant American soldier noted in 1846 that the only glass windows in the province were those in the Palace of the Governors in Santa Fe.

There were three ways to treat window openings. One was to put vertical wood spindles, or bars, into a simple wood frame and cover the frame with cloth or hides to keep out the weather. Another was to use wood shutters to seal the opening, and the third was to use sheets of mica set in a sash with adobe plaster, or set directly into the adobe wall and plastered in. The cloth used to cover the framed openings was a kind of cotton fabric called "lienzo" which transmitted little light but did keep out the wind. Mica, sometimes called isinglass, that is translucent and abounds in the region, was mined in sheets up to 10 by 18 inches in size. Mica panes did not admit much light, but they were more durable than cloth.[30]

After the walls were erected, the roof applied and the doors and windows set in place, the exterior plastering could begin. It became traditional that the women of the congregation applied the plaster. They were called "enjarradoras." Fr. José Garcia, the pastor from 1937 to 1944, wrote in his article, "Symphony in Mud": "For plastering in the Ranchos tradition is women's work; it is the rule and naught can change it—it is correct. The actual plastering is the end that crowns the work."[31] The men mixed the earth, water and straw and brought it to the plasterers. The plaster mixture was the same as was used in the manufacture of the adobe brick with maybe a little more water and finer straw added to make it workable. The plaster was usually applied in three coats: a rough coat placed directly on the adobe walls, a leveling coat and then a final coat applied and smoothed with sheep's wool to a very smooth, hard finish called an "aliz." The women worked from ladders and scaffolds which are shown in several of the photographs and in Imhof's drawing, Illustration 2:3. The scaffold was made using two long logs set about four feet apart that leaned against the wall and supported a wooden platform on top. This method of plastering continues today but with the help of modern equipment.

The interior walls had base courses of adobe plaster similar to the exterior, but in order to lighten the dimly lit church the final coat was made from native

*2:2—The hill southwest of Ranchos de Taos where material for plaster was found. 1991. Photograph by Corina Santistevan.*

gypsum deposits. Almost every settlement and pueblo had a local source of some kind of white gypsum. The material used for interior plastering in the Taos Valley came from a hill southwest of the Santa Fe highway about four miles west of Ranchos de Taos. So much material has been removed through the years that a small cave which was created in the hillside has collapsed. It is no longer used as a source for the white plaster coat.[32] An analysis of the substance by Dr. Rod Ewing of the Geology Department at the University of New Mexico revealed that it was 90 percent quartz, kaolinite and muscovite. Kaolinite is a fine white clay, called "terra alba," used in ceramics and refractories, and ideal for plaster. Muscovite is the most common form of mica which gives a sparkle to the finished wall surface.[33]

The raw material removed from the quarry was pulverized and mixed with a paste of flour and water to make a whitewash, variously called "jaspe," "gesso," "yeso" or just "gypsum." The local people referred to it as "tierra blanca." The thin coating was applied smoothly and evenly over the adobe plaster base and when it became dirty or cracked another coat was put on. Using a magnifying glass , one may count ten coats on the walls of the old plaza buildings. The fresh plaster smelled very clean and good and it was so tasty that children liked to lick it off the walls.[34] The application was again done by the women of the church using soft woolly sheepskin pads in a manner known by the Moors. Sometimes around the base of the wall, two feet or more in height, a dado, also called a wainscot, was sometimes painted with a thin coat of plaster of a darker color using what colored earth was available in the area. A dado about four feet high that came just to the sill of the nave windows was in place in 1934 when the HABS drawings were made. The surveyors called it "tierra amarilla."[35] Sometimes crushed mica was blown onto the wet plaster to make it sparkle. Various designs were often worked around door and window openings.

Interior illumination, other than the light coming in through the small windows and open doors, was by candles set in wooden cross-beam chandeliers called "arañas," on wall brackets, on the altars and the stations of the cross. Sometimes leather lamps covered with mica were used. Domínguez described one at the San Gerónimo de Taos mission as being well made and covered with so much mica that it had a silver sheen.[36] When the altars were being restored in St. Francis in 1980 some candleholders made of adobe were found on top of one of the retables.[37]

Until manufactured pot-bellied iron stoves were brought into New Mexico around 1860, heating for houses came from fireplaces. There is no evidence of fireplaces having been built in churches based on excavation of seventeenth-century and later ones. Churches were without heat until stoves were installed as

*2:3—The one stove was the only heat in the main body of the church, 1934. James Slack Photographer, HABS Collection, Prints and Photographic Division, Library of Congress.*

is shown in the HABS Photographs 2:3 and 2:4. The stoves were usually set toward the front of the nave in the center aisle. One may wonder why such an important item as the stove was not shown on the HABS drawings.

Eighteenth-century Franciscans spoke of the holy oils congealing and the holy water fonts freezing during severe winter cold.[38] The Spanish colonists were a hardy, very religious people to brave the cold weather, walk to the church, sit on the floor or stand in a cold, dark nave during mass and lengthy sermons, and then walk back home afterwards. They surely brought animal skins, blankets and furs with them to ward off the chill.

In the history of many churches the bells have played a very important role, but not so at St. Francis. Little is known about the first bells: where they came from, who made them or what happened to them. The 1831 inventory indicates that the people had paid to have one bell made "with a new clapper."[39] On April 25, 1938, Anthony Gerken wrote Father Garcia that a bolt holding one of the bells broke and the bell crashed to the tower floor. It happened on Easter Sunday after all the services were over. The bell was repaired and put back in place.[40] Father Garcia mentioned in a letter to Archbishop Rudolph A. Gerken, dated December 18, 1938, that the "extra" bell mentioned in the old inventories had been lost.[41] A note on Sheet 1 of the 1934 HABS drawings says, "The original bell has been removed and replaced with a modern bell."[42] Gus Fernandez remembered the "beautiful loud bell" (which may have been one of the original ones, possibly the one bought in 1831) breaking sometime in the 1940's. It was so damaged when it was being repaired that it could never be used again.[43]

Mabel Dodge Luhan almost bought one of the bells. She wrote, "The bells in the low towers of these churches and chapels were secured with difficulty. The one that was in the Ranchos church when I came had been hauled up from Old Mexico, where it had been welded of copper and the contributions of jewelry sent down from here by the women. A few years ago the Ranchos people decided they wanted a new bell, and offered to sell this one for a few hundred dollars. I had not the money then, and Gerson Gusdorf bought it and hung it in the lobby

*2:4—The white line across the ceiling above the choir loft is cloth which was being tacked between the vigas to protect the choir from the dirt on the roof which filtered through the ceiling boards, 1934. James Slack photographer, HABS Collection, Prints and Photographic Division, Library of Congress.*

of the Don Fernando, where it kept company with the corbels and beams from the Taos church until the hotel burned down."[44] It is now in the Kit Carson House.

There was a "camposanto," a wall-enclosed churchyard, built with the original church because it is mentioned in the 1831 inventory as being 22 by 19 varas. Between then and 1856 it had grown to 40 by 22 varas which is 110 by 60 and a half feet, but there were still only the two gates in the front.[45] One of the earliest known photographs, 1:7, shows the pair of front gates with a covered lintel much like it is today. As late as 1934 there were still only the gates in the front, but sometime later, possibly after the rectory was completed, a gate was put in the northeast wall. Also a gate was inserted in the southwest wall near the sacristy after the outside door was moved inside the churchyard. Burials began to be made in the yard after the ban on burials within the church in the middle 1800's. Early photographs show many grave-markers in various locations.

Certain donations and contributions toward the construction and furnishing of the church are documented: Don Ignacio Durán donated the carved double entrance doors and, with Fray Pereyro, the reredos screen. The side-altarpiece which stands in the northeast transept was built and painted at the expense of Don Policarpio "Carpio" Cordova who also paid for the statues of Nuestro Señor de Esquipulas and two other santos, Our Lady of Sorrows and Saint Lydwine from Holland. Don Francisco Martin gave the altar in the southwest arm of the transept which was dedicated to Saint Joseph.[46] In 1953 a former sacristan said that they had been bought "maybe thirty years ago by a rich American." There are eight unassembled panels in the collection of the Denver Art Museum which may be this altar screen which may have been painted by Molleno.[47]

The 1817 inventory describes the interior furnishings when the church was new. "Said Rev. Father (Pereyro) and don Ignacio Durán, and the citizens had built at their cost the (main) altarpiece and had it painted using scaffolding." It is still in place. Photograph 6:1 shows how it looked in 1934 and Photograph 6:2 how it looks today. The parish household had given the statue of Saint Francis which stood in a niche, and the wooden altar table, altar steps and altar rail. The altarpiece in the northeast arm of the sacristy, which is larger than the main altarpiece, was also given by Don Policarpio Cordova and Lorenzo Cordova.[48] See HABS Sheets 16 and 17 for details of it and Sheet 32, which is an ink drawing with applied watercolor of the altarpiece.

There is still uncertainty about many things pertaining to the construction of the church. Is there a stone foundation or were the walls just built on the ground surface? Was the sacristy built at the same time as the main church? When were the buttresses added? These are a only a few of the unanswered questions. Perhaps other documents will be found someday, or future archaeological studies will cast more light on the early architectural history of the church of St. Francis.

## *CHAPTER 3— CHANGES TO THE CHURCH 1813–1967*

Ranchos de Taos was made a parish in 1937 and Father José A. Garcia, a native New Mexican, was the first priest assigned to it. Garcia wrote in 1940, "...the church (Saint Francis of Assisi) has taken well to the modern trimmings, and with no violent renovations, has adopted to herself gradually the changes made throughout the years..."[1] The changes made from the time the church was built up until 1940 in most cases improved the appearance of the building. Repairs were made in close harmony with the past construction, as was true until the major remodeling took place in 1967 when cement stucco replaced the traditional mud plaster.

As I have noted, tradition has it that the church was built like a fortress with small high windows, heavy carved front doors and only a trap door to the roof. It was not until the threat of the Comanche and Ute raiders had been removed after the American occupation that large windows and a less formidable pair of front doors could be considered. Sometime between 1850 and 1860 Wilfred Barton Witt built a lumber mill on Six Mile Creek in the Moreno Valley and mill work became available in the Taos area.[2] Shortly after that, new front doors were installed in the church.

This coincides with the introduction of French priests into New Mexico by Bishop Jean-Baptiste Lamy. When Mexico won its freedom from Spain in 1821, all Spanish friars were ordered from the country. This decree affected the Spanish Franciscans in New Mexico who had charge of the churches in twenty Indian pueblos and one hundred and two towns and ranches. The Bishop of Durango found it impossible to fill their places and the situation worsened until the American occupation in 1846. After the Diocese of Santa Fe was created and Bishop Lamy installed in August, 1851, he began to recruit priests in France and persuade them to come to this so different frontier place. One of the first things these new priests were instructed to do was to repair the long neglected churches, decorate them and supply them with new vestments, altar furniture, linens and other necessities.[3] The first French priest assigned to Taos was Father Gabriel Ussel who came to assume his duties in 1858. There is little doubt that he or one of his successors designed the Gothic style entrance that is in place today. The beautiful doors with the finely designed panel above the transom bar that replaced the original high, carved front doors were very carefully made using milled lumber and trim and in some places peeled round willow branches. These new doors were set forward of the doors they replaced and the existing lintels were left in place. In 1934 the HABS surveyors described the doors (which may

*3:1—This is one of the earliest photographs I have found of the church. St. Francis of Assisi Church Archives.*

not have been the same doors installed around 1860 or the ones shown in the earliest photographs) as being in poor condition, but relatively new. They said the doors appeared to be a combination of rough mill work and hand-run moldings. In some places the moldings had shrunk leaving wide cracks; in other places they were loose and broken, and some molding was missing. In all probability the doors described in 1934 were the doors in place in 1967, having been repaired through the years.[4]

In the photograph above the inscription on the cross is unreadable and appears not to have been painted for some time. It was probably made about the same time as Photograph 1:7, since they both show the small high window in the nave. This proves that the large windows we have today were not put in place until after the front doors were installed and maybe well after. The round corners of the print indicate that it might have been made from a lantern slide. Sometime after the original doors were replaced, the existing window openings in the nave were increased in height and possibly width, and a new mill-made sash was installed as late as 1890. If the window openings were widened the lintels would have had to be replaced which would have been a major construction project. Photograph 3:1 shows a small high window in the southwest wall of the nave which was, no doubt, duplicated in the opposite wall. It is impossible to estimate the width because of the angle of the photograph. The present windows are a fixed sash and have a semi-circular transom which is fitted into a squared wood surround that is set under the lintels. The sash and muntins are mill made. The French priests were familiar with the round arched openings in the Romanesque churches in their country and no doubt found that style of window more attractive and adaptable to the square opening than a Gothic window would have been. All the glass in the windows has been replaced since no glass of the type made in the last century is to be seen today. When the HABS survey was made in early 1934 the transom in the window in the southwest wall of the nave had been removed and the opening boarded up, obviously for repair or replacement. In 1967 the windows were found to be in relatively good condition, but the sills had to be replaced and some minor repair work done to the frames. The windows and doors are carefully detailed on HABS drawings 19 through 26.[5]

It is quite probable that the buttresses, whose forms have made the church the beautiful edifice it is today, were not part of the original design. It is conceivable that not too long after the church was built enough large cracks were visible to the parishoners to cause them to be concerned about the stability of the structure. Adding buttresses was the most logical way to stabilize the walls. The builders could have accomplished their purpose by using smaller buttresses, but fortunately for the beauty of the church they built big ones. There are buttresses against the walls of many of the early New Mexico churches such as Chimayo, Santa Ana, Isleta and Abo. Only at the church of San Gregorio at Abo, built around 1630, are the buttresses an integral part of the structure; at the others they all seem to have been added to solve a structural problem. The people of Ranchos then had examples to draw upon when they were looking for a solution for the stabilization of the walls.[6]

The buttresses built on either side of the main entrance took the thrust of the walls of the nave, while the ones against the walls of the northeast arm of the transept countered the movement of those walls where cracks had occurred. The low walls of the sacristy, with the help of the small buttress at the northwest corner, were sufficient to resist movement in that direction. The large buttress against the northwest-facing apse, which has become the most singular feature of the church, resists the thrust from those walls.

During the 1967 remodeling most of the existing mud plaster on the buttresses was found to be in poor condition and it was removed down to the adobe brick before the new cement stucco was applied. It was observed that there was no bond between the adobe brick in the buttresses and the walls they abutted. This is shown in the photograph of the buttress to the right of the main entrance and was true of all of them.

Kubler thought the function of the buttresses could have been accomplished with less material and more commonplace shapes; but they seemed to satisfy certain formal rather than structural needs. At Ranchos de Taos they certainly soften the contours of the walls and amplify the silhouette of the church.[7] From the earliest known photographs until the 1979 rebuilding of the buttresses there appears to have been very little change in their appearance. In all probability the buttresses that were removed in 1979 were the original ones. The 1979 workers built the new ones to the old shapes and contours as closely as possible.

Maybe at the same time the buttresses were added, the deflection in the beams supporting the high walls at the clerestory windows, the opening over the sanctuary, and the choir loft were seen to be causing problems. The details on Sheets 14 and 20 of the HABS drawings show clearly how supports were in-

*3:2—That there was no bond between the buttresses and the main walls of the church is clearly shown in this 1967 photograph of the buttress on the right side of the front doors. This is typical of all of the buttresses and supports the idea that they were added after the church was built when the walls began to show signs of lateral movement. Photograph by Stan Moore.*

stalled. At the crossing between the nave and the sanctuary with the transept engaged columns were added at the corners of the walls and notched to support diagonal braces. No doubt they were placed on buried stone foundations. The columns added at the transept, or crossing, are milled timbers measuring about eight and one-quarter inches in each dimension. They must have been installed after the arrival of the sawmill in the Taos area around 1860. The columns under the choir loft, however, are round posts. Maybe they were not put in at the same time as those at the crossing. However, both the round and square columns have round carved capitals. The HABS surveyors noted that all of the capitals, corbels and beams were carved and the incised carvings had been painted with red and blue paint. At some time all of the exposed wood had been covered with a

*3:3—The removal of the plaster around the window in the southwest wall of the nave revealed a separation in the wall that was several inches wide and extended several feet horizontally on both sides of the window. This led to the reinforcement of the wall with three vertical steel plates on each side of the window, inside and out, about five feet apart and as high as the bottom of the transom. They are held in place with through-the-wall bolts. Photograph by George Wright.*

white wash which they called "caliche wash."[8] A double corbel was set in the center of each of the spans underneath the supporting beams and then braces were cut to fit tightly into the configuration of the corbels. Similar bracing can be seen in the mission church of Nuestra Señora de Guadalupe in Juarez, Mexico.[9]

In 1967, after the mud plaster was removed, large vertical cracks running from the ground through the top of the parapet were found in almost all of the walls. There was a large void in the southwest-facing wall of the nave which is shown in Photograph 3:3. This may have been caused by pressure on the wall which caused the outer course of adobe to be pushed away from the inner courses, or it may have been built that way deliberately. This is doubtful since the same situation was not seen on the northeast wall of the nave. Movement occurs in all old adobe buildings that were constructed on shallow stone foundations or directly on the ground. The expansion and contraction of the supporting soils, as they absorb moisture and then dry out, cause the walls of the building to rise and subside accordingly. Uneven raising and lowering causes even more stress within the walls and may cause separation of the adobe walls even when they are bonded together since adobe bricks have very little tensile strength.

The earliest changes are undocumented, so I can only conjecture as to how and when they were made. Possibly the first was the addition of the sacristy on the northwest corner of the church. In the early inventories there is mention of a "sacristy" and also of a chest, without a lock, that held the vestments. The writers may not have been referring to a room, but to the location of the chest, say in a corner of the transept. There is some evidence that the present sacristy was built as an addition to the church.

The Historic American Buildings Survey (HABS) drawings show the thickness of the sacristy walls to be from 14 to 18 inches, the latter dimension being the length of the adobe brick found in the buildings that formed the perimeter of the plaza of Ranchos de Taos which was built from 1776 to 1779. This would indicate the addition was made while adobes were still being made to those dimensions, not too long after the church itself was finished.

*3:4—This photograph was made around 1900 by an employee of William Henry Jackson, the famous photographer of the West, who owned the Detroit Photographic Company. The large white cross in front of the church is missing. The vertical boards have been removed from the towers and the nail-grounds have been straightened. Photograph by George E. Mellen, who was a photographer with the Detroit Photographic Company. Courtesy of the Museum of New Mexico. Negative number 104735.*

There is no bond between the sacristy walls and the walls of the church, but that may not indicate later construction because the early builders sometimes did not bond masonry at corners and intersections of walls. The access to the sacristy is awkward but it is probably the best the builders could work out unless they wanted to add as much as two feet of earth fill to bring the floor up to the level of the floor in the church. The question is up for debate: when was the sacristy built?

The earliest photographs show the sacristy in place and Photograph 3:4 shows vigas protruding through the southeast-facing wall indicating they spanned from northwest to southeast. Photograph 3:5 shows that they

*3:5—When this photograph was taken in the late 1800's, the church was being made ready for replastering. The vigas that protruded from the sacristy in Photograph 3:4 have been changed to run the way they do today, southwest to northeast. The grave markers do not seem to be protected. Courtesy of Kit Carson Historic Museums.*

had been changed to span in the opposite direction. When Father Garcia wrote "Symphony in Mud" in 1940 he mentioned the "new sacristy" when he listed the changes to the church known to him.[10] We know from the HABS survey that new vigas and a roof were placed over the sacristy in 1916.[11] It may have been remodeled at that time, certainly with fresh plaster and maybe a new wood floor. Was that what Father Garcia was talking about, or did he mean a sacristy built many years before, but new to the old church? The HABS drawings of 1934 show the vigas are supported on the transept side, not by the walls of the church, but by a post and beam system with the posts sitting on their own foundations.[12]

Another very old photograph is 3:6 which shows the cross faded and some window panes missing. This photograph by Aaron B. Craycraft was made after the completion of the mud plastering. Craycraft may have come to New Mexico as early as 1890 from Illinois. He had a studio on the west side of the plaza in Santa Fe as late as 1904.[13]

Photograph 3:7, made by the Detroit Photographic Company and attributed to William Henry Jackson, the famous expeditionary photographer of the West,

*3:6—This picture may have been taken as early as 1890 after a new coat of plaster had been applied. The work probably was not complete since window panes are missing and ladders are leaning against the wall. Most grave markers have disappeared. Photograph by Aaron B. Craycraft. Courtesy of the Museum of New Mexico. Negative number 9732.*

*3:7—This photograph was taken by William Henry Jackson or one of his staff, perhaps George Mellen, 1885–1900. Colorado Historical Society. Negative number WHJ 40270.*

may have been made as early as 1885. This picture of the front facade of the church shows that the bell towers in place at that time were made of adobe and were very much in the configuration we see today. Some years earlier, before the large nave windows were installed, the bell towers were seen to be obviously deteriorating so wood headers, or grounds, probably 2" by 8" in size, had been attached to the adobe walls of the towers to support vertical wood boards which were applied later. When this picture was made the boards were being replaced. There is a hole in the roof of the southwest bell tower which is a wood structure with overlapping boards for the roof. The ladder leaning against the nave wall suggests that repair work was in progress. A new, larger cross has been installed in front of the church and it is mounted without any diagonal braces. The missing window panes seem to have been replaced. The large crowd assembled for some special occasion, maybe a wedding.

Since their exposed location made the towers more vulnerable to the damaging erosion of rain and snow than the rest of the church, someone may have decided that cladding them with wood would provide the needed protection. Obviously aesthetics were not being considered. I have found nothing in the written records about this work. The unanswered questions are: when were the boards first applied and when were they replaced? Why did not one of the French priests design more interesting wooden towers such as they did at San Augustín Church at Isleta or San Felipe de Neri in Albuquerque?

Some people must have liked the appearance of the towers with the board siding because a photograph of San Gerónimo Church in Taos Pueblo, made probably before 1920, shows a single bell tower in the center of the front facade that is very similar to the ones at St. Francis. It was probably done by the same priest. (Photograph 3:9)

Fray Marius Joseph Giraud, affectionately known as Father Joe, was the priest at the parish of Our Lady of Guadalupe in Taos from 1904 to 1934 and served the mission church at Ranchos de Taos during those thirty years. Mabel Dodge Luhan knew and wrote about him. She said he was from Lyon and was a very practical man. She described him as having a kind of geniality about him, and he was cheerful and convivial. Giraud had a square black beard and wore thick glasses which Mabel said made him appear inscrutable. He drove about in a high buggy with two black horses and a driver who helped him in the church and rectory. Some time later he bought a shiny black Buick.

*3:8—A detail of the newly applied boards on the walls of one of the bell towers. Note the outline of the adobe wall behind the boards. Photograph by Wesley Bradfield. Courtesty of the Museum of New Mexico. Negative number 148453.*

*3:9—San Gerónimo Church, Taos Pueblo, shows a bell tower similar to those at Ranchos de Taos. Courtesy of the Museum of New Mexico. Negative number 4423.*

*3:10—The date on the cross is March, 1915, and it appears to be recently painted. Courtesy Kit Carson Historic Museums.*

*3:11—A photograph by Oscar Berninghaus made sometime before 1915. Courtesy of Kit Carson Historic Museums.*

*3:12—This photograph had a note with it saying it was made in 1915 after the towers had been "remuddied." Photograph by Oscar Berninghaus. Courtesy of Kit Carson Historic Museums.*

Giraud lived on the street behind the church where he created a bit of France for himself. He had a large garden laid out in the provincial French manner with long neat rows of vegetables and square beds of various kinds of flowers from roses to hollyhocks. In the rear there were fruit trees and berry vines. A small corral held a few sheep to provide meat for his table. Mabel had lunch one day in Father Joe's house and described him as being very much the French curé. He poured red wine, which he had made himself, from a glass pitcher into tumblers and she said his face reddened more and more as the meal proceeded. And a good meal it was, with a leg of lamb, fresh peas, a crisp French salad with lots of garlic and a round brown loaf of very good bread.[14]

As soon as he arrived in Taos, Giraud tore off the old roof on Our Lady of Guadalupe church and put on a pitched corrugated metal roof. He threw out all the corbels and they wound up in Gusdorf's Don Fernando Hotel which later burned to the ground. However, because of the close involvement of the people in St. Francis of Assisi church, he made only a few necessary changes to it during his thirty-year tenure.

One of the most striking changes was the removal of the boards on the bell towers and the repair, reroofing and replastering of the towers. Father Giraud was also responsible for the installation of precast concrete coping stones on top of the main walls of the church that protected the walls from erosion to some extent. Giraud also built a stairway to the choir loft to replace the old ladder, put down a new wood floor, repaired the spalling plaster, replaced the sacristy and transept vigas, and reroofed the entire church, the latter work being done around 1930.[15]

Father Giraud was a sensitive person so removing the boards from the bell towers and restoring them to something like their original design must have been a priority with him. There is no way to determine when the boards were first applied, but we can pinpoint when they were finally removed thanks to two photographs made by Oscar Berninghaus, a noted Taos artist. (Photographs 3:11 and 3:12.) Notes with the negative of the picture showing the boards in place say that it was made in "early 1915." The note with the second negative says that it was made a little bit later in 1915 and "...the towers have been remuddied." Berninghaus did a painting of the church

*Illustration 3:1—This drawing by Ralph M. Pearson is dated December, 1919, and is one of the few drawings or photographs that is accurately dated. Courtesy of Kit Carson Historic Museums.*

while the facing-boards were in place and it shows they were painted white.[16]

Sometime, probably in the 1920's, a friend of Mabel's, Bobby Jones, a Broadway producer who was visiting her, was at the church and found a number of spindles from the choir loft railing that had been removed. A new railing had probably been installed at the same time the ladder to the choir loft was replaced with a stair. He picked up the spindles and he and Mabel built them into the main gate to the Luhan house where they remain to this day.[17]

The methods and materials used in the construction of the first roof on the church have been described previously. From the very beginning, keeping the roof watertight must have been a serious problem. Even the advent of the tar, or asphalt, and gravel built-up roofs did not wholly remedy the situation. The dates of some of the roof repairs done in this century have been recorded and mentioned above. When the sacristy and transept vigas were replaced around 1916 a new roof was applied. The HABS notes say a new ceiling was put over the existing vigas in the nave between 1924 and 1933, most likely before the reroofing around 1930.[18]

There was a change made to the church that may have occurred during Father Giraud's time or before. In Photograph 3:10 there are the ends of vigas protruding through the southeast wall of the transept next to the sacristy. The date on the cross is March, 1915. The viga ends do not appear in later photographs. What did they hold up? There may have been a small choir loft built over the entrance to the sacristy that held only a few people who participated in an "antiphonal" choir arrangement. The loft could not have extended across the transept because it would have interfered with the St. Joseph altar in place on the northwest wall at that time, so it

*3:13—Gates at Mabel Dodge Luhan's house with the spindles from the choir loft railing that was removed from Saint Francis of Assisi church. Photograph by the author. 1993.*

3:14—The front doors of the church around 1930. Photograph by Wharton Huber. Courtesy of the Museum of New Mexico. Negative number 142395.

must have been supported by a post set in the middle of the transept.

When Father Garcia came to St. Francis in 1937, he took great pride in the church and soon began to make much needed repairs. A letter to Archbishop Rudolph A. Gerken written on July 1, 1938, stated that planning was proceeding to replaster the church and make some roof repairs. He noted one visible bad crack and suspected more would be uncovered when the plaster was removed. He asked the Archbishop to have his architect, meaning John Gaw Meem, stop by and give advice about repairing the church particularly if he did find more cracks.[19]

Meem had practiced architecture in New Mexico from his office in Santa Fe since 1924 and had done several projects for the archdiocese. In the 1920's he had been very active in the Society for the Preservation and Restoration of New Mexico Mission Churches and had acquired a reputation for repairing and restoring adobe structures. The Archbishop referred the request to Meem who replied immediately that he would be delighted to help in any way possible.[20]

Feeling relieved that he had professional help if needed, Garcia proceeded with the removal of the plaster. He wrote Archbishop Gerken on August 9, 1938, "The replastering of the Ranchos Church started this week. The old plaster is all off. Several cracks were uncovered, but they are all old ones—the reason why the buttresses were originally built. Common opinion is that they extend only to the first or second layer of adobes. We will fill bad cracks with adobe and proceed. I am starting this so as not to have Mr. Meems (sic) make a useless trip. I can describe the cracks to him in case I should ever see him. They do not look too dangerous. The main one runs down in a narrow line 15 feet from the coping. Apparently an old one. It was probably helped along a little by water seeping down from under the cement coping, and also by the swallow

3:15—The date on the cross is March, 1915, but it must have been there a long time since the church walls are now badly in need of replastering. A canopy was built over the clerestory window either to reduce the amount of light and heat coming down on the sanctuary or to stop water leaks. Courtesy of the Museum of New Mexico. Negative number 59267.

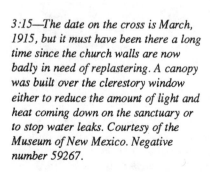

nests, as it was popular for apartments for them. It is on the north side-chapel, and the two big buttresses this side were apparently built to keep it from spreading. It apparently affects only the first layer of adobes. The others are smaller. The new plastering will protect them."[21] Enough information was passed to Meem that he could write to Garcia on August 15 expressing delight that he was replastering with mud and doing it in the old fashioned way using women who traditionally have always done this work. He assured Garcia that he was doing the work correctly by filling the old cracks. He wrote, "The great problem in all adobe buildings is to keep the water out and by filling the cracks up, you will eliminate the danger of increasing the size of the cracks." Meem offered to come to Ranchos de Taos if Garcia ran into serious problems, but he never had to make the trip.[22]

Reverend Paul V. Hatch was pastor from 1947 until 1954 and during that time he saw several repairs made to the church. He wrote Archbishop Byrne to tell him that the church had been re-roofed in September, 1949, and also said, "...(the church) is now being 'remudded,' or whatever you would call giving it a new coat of mud and straw. The same thing will be done to the rectory next week. An average of 4 or 5 voluntary workers have been engaged in this work for two weeks." Hatch wrote to Byrne again on March 8, 1950, saying, "When I came here the condition of the old church was such that if something was not done to it within a very short time it would have collapsed. It is now in a condition that ought to guarantee its existence for many years to come although it will need a new floor in the not too distant future."[23]

That the contours of the exterior walls have changed little through the years is shown by various photographs and the HABS drawings. In the plastering process, which also doesn't seem to have changed very much, if the old plaster is in poor condition it is all scraped off the walls down to the adobe brick and new plaster is applied in approximately the same thickness as before. If the plaster is in reasonably good condition and adhering well to the walls it is left in place and only a new finish coat applied. Replastering has been done sporadically through the years. Looking at old photographs it is clear that the plaster was often allowed to get in very poor condition before it was redone. Some pictures, such as Number 3:15, made be-

*3:16—Through the years the job of replastering the church was done by women called "enjarradoras." This picture, believed to have been taken around 1940, shows the women mixing the mud and straw with water to make the plaster. Kit Carson Historic Museums.*

*3:17—The women worked from both ladders and scaffolds while plastering the church. Kit Carson Historic Museums.*

*3:18—Scaffolding on the front of St. Francis of Assisi church around 1940. Kit Carson Historic Museums.*

*3:19—The "enjarradoras" are plaster-ing the front of the church while men are erecting scaffolding on the southwest wall. Note the new larger bell. The vigas have been removed from the southeast facing wall next to the sacristy. Courtesy of the Museum of New Mexico, Negative 74485.*

tween 1915 and 1920, show the exterior walls in a very bad state of neglect. Father Garcia wrote in his article, "Symphony in Mud," that they were replastering the church for the ninth time since it was built. This means that up to 1940 there had been an average of 14 years between plasterings. How did he know how many times it had been plastered since records of such things were not carefully kept?[24]

Reverend Clarence F. Galli became the pastor at St. Francis in 1958 and he also took a strong interest in keeping the church buildings in good repair, even though he was accused by a Taos resident of having had the windows of the church painted by amateurs and not understanding the considerable importance of the church. He early on had to remove the buttresses from the school gymnasium because of water damage. They were rebuilt using reinforced concrete block.[25] In 1961 he was informing Archbishop Byrne of the need for a new floor and pews in the church.[26] He was told in May that if he raised one-half of the money needed he could proceed with the work. Galli obtained a bid on a new wood floor of $7,259, so he recommended going to a concrete slab instead that would only cost $1,887. John McHugh, a Santa Fe architect, had suggested using brick set on sand, but concrete was the final choice.[27] The floor slab followed the slope of the old wood floor which, no doubt, had followed the original dirt floor. A concrete slab was also placed in the choir loft over the existing wood floor.[28]

Gustavo Fernandez was given the job of building new pews so he found an illustration in a catalog of church furniture that he thought harmonized with the interior feeling of St. Francis and built the pews based on the picture. When he began to install the pews he found they intruded on the center aisle as he set them from the back of the church forward. He had not recognized the subtle inward slope of the nave walls from the back to the crossing. Unfortunately, he had to do a lot of cutting and fitting to make the sides of the center aisle straight.[29]

*3:20—The church after the replastering was completed circa 1940. New Mexico State Tourist Bureau. Negative number 20036.*

In late 1965, Monsignor Francis J. Reinberg of the office of the archdiocese expressed his concern about the poor condition of the church. He advised the pastor, Father Manuel Alvarez, not to do anything to repair the roof until he had an architect or engineer look at the whole church. He said, "It is a venerable mission type building with national renown, and we must at all costs, keep it in good shape." This action led to the major remodeling that took place in 1966–67.[30]

An interesting feature, which has nothing to do with the church building itself, is the appearance in even the oldest known photograph of a large white cross sitting in the middle of the walkway through the churchyard. The wording on the cross has changed a little but "Recuerdo de la Mision," or sometimes it is spelled "Micion," is painted on it with dates. After talking with Father O'Brien and others, I learned the meaning of the cross and the inscriptions. At various times a missionary priest is brought in to deliver sermons over a period of several days to restore the religious spirit of the congregation. The words mean "Remember the Mission (of the Church)" and the dates are the time the "revival" was held. The dates helped a great deal in establishing when many of the photographs were made. However, some years elapsed between the meetings and so sometimes the date stayed on the cross a long time. According to Father Walter Cassidy it was the responsibility of the missionary priest to erect the cross.[31]

## *CHAPTER 4—THE 1967 REMODELING*

In the September–October, 1963, issue of *New Mexico Architecture* there was an article by the editor, John Conron, about the poor condition of the mud plaster on the exterior of St. Francis of Assisi Church at Ranchos de Taos. The editor states,

"The parishioners, faced with the perpetual maintenance problems inherent in adobe construction, have decided to protect the church with a coating of stucco. Until now the church has been surfaced in the traditional way with adobe mud plaster which contributes to the beautiful soft contours of the edifice.

"Hard cement plaster, altho (sic) it protects the surface from erosion, destroys the flowing, organic quality which is the visual delight of New Mexico's Colonial buildings. The value of this particular church far outreaches the confines of the small parish responsible for its maintenance. It has become apparent in the past few years that the Archdiocese has been either unable or unwilling to undertake the responsibility for the maintenance of the valuable historical  monument under its jurisdiction. A void exists, which time and the ravages of weather refuse to acknowledge.

"At the moment, the Ranchos church is the one most in need of immediate action. Donations are needed for the expensive process of re-mudding the exterior. Once this immediate task has been accomplished, a long range study of the possibilities of adobe preservation must be undertaken. Some research has been carried on in the areas of applied silicones. More effort must be spent in this field so that the many adobe relics which surround us in this New Mexico country can be retained for the pleasure and education of future generations."

Conron suggested that the New Mexico Chapter of the American Institute of Architects assume responsibility for the research and asked for donations to help defray the expense of plastering the church with mud. There was no response to the plea and the church continued to deteriorate.[1]

In 1966, a contract was let to John Gianardi, a building contractor from Santa Fe, to apply a new roof and do some minor repairs. When he removed the existing roofing, which was in very poor condition, he found there was as much as a foot of dirt fill on top of the roof deck. Upon removing some of the dirt, he discovered that about half the thickness of the deck boards had rotted away and some of the supporting vigas had disintegrated from dry rot to one-half their original diameter. Where the vigas went through the outside supporting walls

4:1—*The front of St. Francis of Assisi church in the fall of 1966. Photograph by Stan Moore.*

less than half the timber remained. This was also true of many of the corbels which penetrated the outside walls. After seeing the dangerous condition of the roof structure, the contractor and the church officials felt some engineering advice was needed.

My involvement with the church began in August, 1966, when Monsignor Francis Reinberg of the Archdiocese of Santa Fe called me. For many years he had been the person on the Archbishop's staff most involved in the administration of the church's building projects. I had worked closely with him on several while I was in private practice. The Monsignor said there was an "engineering" problem at the Ranchos de Taos church and asked me whom I could recommend to do the work. He said there were some problems with the roof. I pointed out the historic significance of the church and suggested that an architect knowledgeable about preservation of historic structures be employed to look at the problem and propose solutions that would not be out of place. At his request I named three firms I thought would be competent. The Archdiocese chose George Wright Associates of Albuquerque for the work. Wright had done several projects for the Archdiocese and the church administrators were familiar with his firm.

4:2—*The southwest side of the church in 1966. Photograph by Stan Moore.*

4:3—The adobe walls were being severely eroded beneath the pre-cast concrete coping. Photograph by Stan Moore.

4:4—The entire church was in need of replastering in 1966. Photograph by Stan Moore.

4:5—This is a close-up view of the condition of the parapets and walls. Photograph by Stan Moore.

4:6—The dirt fill under the roof was shaped to direct the run-off water to the canales. The roofing material was in poor condition and there were several leaks. Photograph by Stan Moore.

4:7—When the contractor removed the several inches of earth fill on the roof, the ceiling boards were found to have rotted almost through and the vigas underneath were also in a dangerous condition. Photograph by George Wright.

On September 9, 1966, Monsignor Reinberg, George Wright, some of Wright's staff and I went to Ranchos de Taos to examine the church building. We met with Father Manuel Alvarez, the pastor, and Gustavo Fernandez, the president of the Parish Council. They explained that in the past the parishioners had replastered the walls of the church every few years. The work was time consuming and since most of the men and many of the women worked they did not want to continue the practice. In fact, they stated that the church was too small and maybe a new church should be built and the existing church turned over to the National Park Service for a national monument or be made into a museum. In any case the church was desperately in need of repairs, so George Wright and his staff began an inspection without waiting for a decision on its future.[2]

After completing his inspection Wright immediately ordered shoring placed under the first five vigas in the nave next to the crossing, the removal of all dirt on the roof and a thorough examination of all the vigas.[3]

After this brief inspection of the church it was decided that the architects should make a complete investigation, prepare a report on the condition of the structure and recommend the necessary steps to repair it.

A few days later the report was presented to Archbishop James Peter Davis with four basic proposals concerning the future of the church:

1. Abandon the church, do nothing to maintain it.
2. Partially restore the church and get by with minimal repairs.
3. Turn the church over to the National Park Service for designation as a national monument.
4. Start a full-fledged program of restoration and maintenance.

The report contained specific recommendations if the fourth proposal was accepted, such as: replacing the badly rotted vigas and roof deck; replacing the earth fill on the roof deck with light weight insulation and improving the roof drainage pattern; either stuccoing the exterior walls or mud-plastering them and treating the mud-plaster with a chemical weather-proofing agent; rebuilding the bell towers; recessing all exposed electrical wiring into the walls; protecting the buttresses; replacing the confessionals; and installing a new heating system.[4]

Archbishop Davis decided to begin the program of restoration and maintenance and agreed to provide funding. Gianardi was employed to do the restoration work.

4:8—*The vigas which ran through the parapets were also rotten. Photograph by Stan Moore.*

4:9—*The apse of the church with the old mud plaster removed. The white material on the walls is a harder substance which may have been a caliche or kaolinite plaster mixture from a cave some miles southwest of the church. Photograph by George Wright.*

4:10:—*When the adobe plaster was removed from the northeast wall, a crack was found running from the ground through the parapet. Photograph by George Wright.*

4:11—Extensive repairs had to be made to the bell towers. Photograph by Stan Moore.

4:12—The nave window in the northeast wall. Photograph by George Wright.

After further investigation it became apparent that all the vigas as well as several of the corbels would have to be replaced because of their badly rotted condition. Vigas of the required diameter were not on hand and because of the lateness of the season they could not be cut and hauled out of the forests. Gianardi found some logs at a mill near Eagle Nest that had been cut for utility poles and could be used for the roof vigas. Unfortunately they had already been treated with creosote. It was imperative to finish the roof before winter set in, so the creosoted logs were installed and the rotted corbels replaced at the same time. The vigas were donated by the Angel Fire Ski Resort.[5]

In a report made on January 29, 1967, Kent Stout, an associate of George Wright, noted that upon entering the church there was a strong odor of creosote. The unpleasant odor persisted for a long time until a chemical deodorant was found that seemed to remove the smell.[6] It is not noticeable today.

On February 2, 1967, the *Taos News* ran a story with the headline: "Church Restoration Stirs Passions" and a sub-heading: "Controversy Swarms Over Hardplastering" (sic). The article quoted Fr. Alvarez as saying, "After long study and consideration by the Archbishop and the architects, we have decided that the church must be hardplastered." He said the decision was reached because of the difficulty in modern times of finding persons who can put on the soft plaster. The article said that the decision had already drawn criticism from The Friends of the Taos Valley and the Spanish Colonial Society in Santa Fe. Ben Hazard, secretary of the Taos organization, had sent a letter of protest to Archbishop Davis saying it was a mistake to hard plaster the "living museum."

E. Boyd, curator of the Spanish Colonial Society, declared that stucco is no more permanent than adobe mud plaster. She cited the example of the Palace of the Governors in Santa Fe, whose north wall collapsed one spring after stuccoing. She also said it would be just as expensive to hard plaster as to continue mud plastering.

Archbishop Davis declined to comment to the reporter. An archdiocesan official explained that he felt it was a local matter which Fr. Alvarez and the parishioners should work out as they saw fit.

J. A. Maes, a member of the St. Francis of Assisi parish, said the parishioners felt the same as Fr. Alvarez did. He said, "In the good old days, people were more willing to get together and do the plastering. Today, it is hard to get people to do it. We don't want to be selfish, but we do have a problem."[7]

On February 3, Genevieve Janssen, chairman of The Friends of Taos Valley association, wrote Archbishop Davis a letter requesting a meeting as soon as possible to discuss the problem. Davis asked George Wright to reply to Ms. Janssen.[8]

A letter was sent to the Archbishop on the sixth by Mrs. Sammy Heaton concerning the proposed establishment of a "Perpetual Maintenance Fund" to assure the continuing use of mud plaster on both the exterior and interior of the church. She proposed setting the fund at between $55,000 and $65,000. She said her "pro-tem committee" had raised $6,846 in pledges in twenty-four hours from fifty-five individuals and families. I have not found a reply to this idea and nothing more seems to have been done.[9] The article reporting on the fund-raising effort in the *Taos News* of the ninth said the final decision concerning the establishment of the fund lay with Archbishop Davis.

This same news story reported that "an interested individual," Frederick Kackley, a student at the Wurlitzer Foundation, had contacted about twenty-five people in the area who indicated they would help with the "mud work." According to Kackley, the controversy over the church plastering had spread to neighboring states, and the faculty and students of the University of Colorado would be interested enough in preserving the building to come to Taos and assist in the work. The article stated that groups which had joined in the drive included the Millicent Rogers Museum, the Kit Carson Historic Museums, the Craftsmen's Guild and the Historical Society of Taos. It further stated that most of these groups and hundreds of private citizens concerned with the fate of the old church had written to the Archbishop.[10]

On the thirteenth Wright replied to Ms. Janssen, pointing out that he had "... recommended that every effort be made to retain the soft mud plaster surface on the exterior if at all possible." He went on to explain that the earth and straw mixture with an admixture for waterproofing would be applied to a portion of the adobe walls for evaluation.[11]

On that same day, Gustavo Fernandez, president of the St. Francis of Assisi Parish Council, wrote Archbishop Davis reiterating the council's decision made at the meeting on the tenth to proceed with the stucco work based on the architect's report in which he "... advises that a coat of hard plaster over a wall secured with wire mesh would, in effect, lend the necessary protection and reinforcement that would be found wanting should soft plaster be applied." The report does not say this exactly, but it does say that a carefully

*4:13—The openings in the towers were constructed with true adobe brick arches. Photograph by Stan Moore.*

*4:14—As the vigas, corbels and ceiling boards were replaced, the masons followed with a concrete block parapet. Photograph by George Wright.*

*4:15—Detail of the construction of the new parapet. Photograph by Stan Moore.*

applied stucco coating could be applied at no great loss to form and appearance. Mr. Fernandez's letter says further that the council was ". . . determined to proceed with the application of permanent hard plaster oblivious to the din and clambor (sic) raised by other well thinking persons."[12]

Wright also said in his report of October 21, 1966, that if the stucco was applied the form and color could be retained, but the earthen quality of the mud plaster would be lost forever. He said that if more time could be allowed to find an agent which would waterproof the mud plaster there might be a solution to the problem. He concluded, "In short, it may not be the wisest course to stucco immediately without further investigation. This phase of the work could be delayed while the roof (was applied) and structural repairs were made." Wright was torn between the demand of the parish council to cover the walls with stucco which they believed would eliminate the need for annual mud plastering and his feeling, shared by many others, that stuccoing would ruin the "feeling" of the building. He summed up his concerns by writing, ". . . as the church is the center of a rapidly growing tourist area, Ranchos de Taos (church) has become the chief jewel in a fabulous scenic and historic crown. Tourists from fifty states and foreign countries come to see, to admire, and to photograph this beautiful building. This living symbol must be preserved for future generations to enjoy as we have enjoyed it in the past, and are still enjoying it today."[13]

In order to keep the mud-plastered exterior and also meet the council's desire for a more maintenance-free wall covering, Wright and his staff began to look for some admixture, or coating, that could be used to make the mud plaster at least water resistant, if not waterproof. Kent Stout, an architect with George Wright Associates, contacted Charles "Chick" Sigler, an architect with the National Park Service then in San Francisco but for many years located in Santa Fe. Sigler referred him to Orvel Johnson, who had retired from the California Division of Public Works, Architecture Branch. Johnson was president of the National Association of Restoration Specialists. Sigler said, "For my part I think the ideal solution is mud plaster, applied as often as necessary. However, I can appreciate the financial burden on the Ranchos parishioners. I get pains in my belly when I think what could happen if water got under the stucco unknownst to all and the adobe walls and/or buttresses disintegrated as happened to the buttresses on the National Park Service building in Santa Fe."[14] How prophetic!

Stout wrote Johnson explaining the problem at Ranchos de Taos and Johnson quickly replied on February 27. He recommended the use of "Acryl-60" or other similar acrylic material mixed with the adobe soil to create a stabilized adobe mix which could be used as plaster. The formula called for one part portland cement to 8 to 10 parts of soil containing about 20% sand by volume, and one part Acryl-60 to three parts water with mineral oxide for color and straw binder added as desired for appearance. Johnson said that water with Acryl-60 should be added to the dry mix until the mud will "just ball" in the hand. He was of the opinion that this plaster should last from fifty to one hundred years! Because of the time pressure and the inability to confirm successful use of this mixture, the recommendation could not be given the consideration it probably deserved. [15]

In the meantime John Gaw Meem had become aware of the project and the plastering problem. On February 8, Meem wrote to Genevieve Janssen in reply to a question she asked him about how to waterproof the mud plaster. He said that he had used a product called "Pencapsula" on the stable and garage at his home in Santa Fe the previous fall with excellent results. He said the process was developed by the National Park Service for use in stabilizing adobe ruins. Meem said, "It would be a fine thing if the Ranchos de Taos church could be treated with this material which will not discolor the adobe and will last a long time (possibly the life of the building)." He estimated the cost to be about fifty cents per square foot applied. [16]

Several of us who were involved in the project, including Monsignor Reinberg, went by and looked at Meem's stable and we all thought it looked very good. There was no discoloration of the plaster so you could not have known anything had been applied except for a slight shine on the exposed straw. We thought this would be the answer to the problem.

The news of the controversy finally reached Albuquerque and on February 23 the *Albuquerque Tribune* carried a brief story under the headline, "Stucco on Taos Church? It's Sacrilegious." The paper quoted The Friends of the Taos Valley as saying, "It should be hand coated with soft adobe mud as it has been for centuries—anything else would be sacrilegious." The Friends also said replacing the vigas and parapet was sacrilegious. [17]

The *Taos News* carried a story on the same day which stated that Nathaniel Owings, a partner in the architectural firm of Skidmore, Owings and Merrill (SOM), who had a home in Pojoaque, New Mexico, had pledged $1,000 to "soft plaster" the church. He suggested possibly using Pencapsula, citing its extensive use by the Park Service. The article said that it had been used on the surface of the adobe ruins at Fort Union National Monument near Las Vegas in 1962. An article in an unnamed national magazine was quoted as having said that the chemical had been successful in protecting the adobe from deterioration. [18]

While the controversy over plaster was raging about the exterior of the church, work was proceeding on the interior. The new heating system was being installed, and the new electrical system was being recessed into the walls. A very attractive wood molding was uncovered on the right side of the nave about four inches below the bottom of the corbels. No matching molding was found on the opposite wall. It represents the "cord of St. Francis" and was often put in churches built by the Francisican Order. The molding was left exposed when the new gypsum plaster was applied.

The concrete floor slab placed in the choir loft around 1960 was removed and replaced with a wood floor because it was overstressing the wood structure beneath. The hard-packed earth floors in the bell towers were removed and

*4:16—All of the loose plaster was removed from the interior walls. Photograph by George Wright.*

*4:17—The exterior walls were covered with scaffolding as the work progressed. Photograph by M. Kent Stout, George Wright Associates.*

*4:18—There was almost no light to work by in the interior except for a few electric lights and what came in through the nave windows. Photograph by Stan Moore.*

replaced with concrete. The new furnace was built into the space below the tower on the southeast corner of the church. While the workmen were removing the earth floors they found the skeletal remains of some infants. The remains were re-interred in the churchyard.

On March 13, Meem wrote George Wright confirming a previous telephone conversation about the use of Pencapsula. After some refiguring Meem's cost estimate had dropped to fifteen and a half cents per square foot. He concluded the letter saying, "Should you decide to use Pencapsula over the traditional 'tierra vallita' adobe walls, I'll be glad to send Father Alvarez $1,000 to help meet the cost as I think its use will set a precedent for the survival of adobe construction in our region."[19]

Early in March Meem had a meeting with Archbishop Davis, and as a result Davis agreed that if a Society for the Preservation of New Mexico Mission Churches, similar to the one that did such effective work in the 1920's, were established, he would not only cooperate but would welcome its help. The archbishop also said he would consider the use of Pencapsula on the church. Unfortunately the Society was not re-established as such, but other similar organizations are supporting efforts to restore not only the mission churches but all old churches.

Meem left on March 21 for a visit with his daughter's family in California, hoping that the mud-plastered exterior of the church would be saved. While in California he sent a telegram to Archbishop Davis asking that the final decision on the exterior treatment be withheld until his return. In a letter to Ms. Janssen, dated April 14, he referred to a meeting held the week after Easter in which the decision was made to use hard plaster in spite of the recommendation of George Wright and himself to try the surface treatment first.

Upon his return Meem spoke with Monsignor Reinberg who told him that the decision to stucco was based mainly on the fact that the Pencapsula treatment was still in the experimental stage and would not solve the parishioners' desire for a permanent installation.

After the decision was made the work proceeded to completion with little more outward opposition even though many people were very disappointed about it.

Meem wrote to Ms. Janssen, "It looks as if we have lost the struggle to keep the exterior of the Ranchos de Taos church in authentic adobe plaster, stabilized with Pencapsula, instead of being covered with hard cement stucco." He concluded with the following paragraph:

"And so, this effort has failed. But considering the tremendous importance of these old missions, historically and culturally, to the American people, we must keep on trying, and the sooner we can get the proposed Society for their preservation under way, the better it will be. And in spite of what is happening to the beautiful old Ranchos de Taos church, I know you and the people of Taos will help get the Society going when the time comes."[20]

As far as I've been able to find, nothing more appeared in the press until August 13, 1967, when an article by Vee Busch was published in the "Sundial" section of the *El Paso Times*, headlined: "Hard Plastering Marks End of Era in Traditional Adobe Architecture." The writer said the change to the church was being mourned by art historians as ". . . the end of another chapter in traditional adobe architecture." She continued: "The essential lines of the church have been preserved and the church has been saved from total decay. But to the adobe 'aficionado' it will never be the same." She quoted an unnamed Taos writer as saying, "The beauty of the church lies in the centuries of hands that have worked on it with love and devotion. To hard plaster the building and hide the work of all those hands robs St. Francis of one of its most powerful aspects." [21]

In a letter written to me in August, 1974, George Wright, then dean of the School of Architecture at the University of Texas at Arlington, made the following comments:

"Looking back on the project, I must say that it was interesting, but I regret that it wasn't handled in a more sympathetic manner. Granted an emergency existed, the roof was in danger of collapsing, still, more time should have been taken to bring in archaeologists to survey the building, weigh the proposals for restoration and consider the offers to raise money from private sources."[22]

*4:19—A mason is repairing the nave wall. Photograph by Stan Moore.*

*4:20—The Franciscan rope molding sits beneath the corbels on the northeast wall of the nave. Note the contrast between the new and the old corbels. Photograph by John Martin Campbell. 1994.*

*4:21—Photograph showing the construction of the choir floor. Photograph by Stan Moore.*

4:22—One of the bell towers after repairs were made and cement stucco applied. Photograph by Stan Moore.

Many other repairs were made to the church which were not as controversial as the plastering of the exterior walls. Besides the new roof structure and other things already mentioned, new confessionals were built; a new stairway to the choir loft was put in to replace the old one, but the newel post was kept; and the entire inside of the church was replastered with gypsum plaster, as in the past.

Not too long after the remodeling was finished the National Park Service stopped using any kind of chemical stabilizers on its adobe buildings because of deleterious effects on the adobe. Later I was told the exterior of Meem's stable began to look like cornflakes. The plaster cracked into small pieces and fell off to the depth the Pencapsula had penetrated.[23]

There was no easy solution to the replastering problem. If it was to be done correctly, it had to be mud plastered by hand in the old fashioned way, as was resumed in 1979 and continued yearly to this day.

4:23—The apse buttress after the stucco was applied. Gone are the soft flowing lines of the mud plaster. Photograph by the author.

4:24—The northwest facade after the stucco work was completed. Photograph by the author. Circa 1970.

## *CHAPTER 5— 1979 REPLASTERING AND BEYOND*

Almost before the stucco application was completed in 1967 it had begun to crack. By 1970 the cracks were so bad, both in the walls of the church and the churchyard, that a painting contractor was hired to put a fiberglass fabric tape over the cracks and then paint the entire building with a fibered paint. The cracks reappeared very quickly, splitting the tape and pulling the fabric loose. There was enough movement in the walls and the stucco to buckle the tape as the openings closed and tear it apart when they opened up again. The surface was repaired several times and the continued patching and painting resulted in a very unsightly surface since the taped joints showed clearly and as the paint color faded it did not, in time, match the color of the stucco.

Father Michael O'Brien, known to his friends and parishioners as "Father Mike," was ordained in Taos in 1970 and said his first mass on June 28 of that year. He always had a fondness in his heart for the old church, so when he was assigned to Ranchos de Taos in 1977 he became interested in restoring the church to its former beauty.

Father O'Brien first had the constitution of the Parish Council rewritten to return the church to the traditional way of governance with mayordomos responsible for the care of the church during one-year non-renewable terms. The mayordomos form the Parish Council: six husband-and-wife couples or sometimes two men or two women from Ranchos de Taos and two couples each from the missions, Talpa, Llano Quemado and Los Cordovas/Cordillera.[1]

In March, 1978, the Santa Fe architectural firm of Johnson Nestor was asked to visit Ranchos de Taos, examine the church, and recommend what should be done to repair it. Robert Nestor inspected the church on March 6, 1978, and reported his findings to Father O'Brien in a letter dated March 22. He said, "The condition of the church at Ranchos de Taos is remarkably good for an adobe building of its age and must be due to the love and care it has received over the years. Exterior stucco is undoubtedly the most serious problem. The exterior cement stucco continues to crack, allowing the erosion which cannot be seen and so cannot be measured. Cracks are in some cases large and running in such a way as to catch water. I could not touch bottom in these cracks with a four inch knife blade indicating that there has been considerable erosion along the crack line or that the stucco has separated from the building in places." He suggested a detailed look at the exterior of the building to determine the extent of stucco

*5:1—In 1979, after the stucco was removed from the buttresses, it was found that the adobe bricks were mostly mud or loose dirt due to water penetration through cracks in the stucco. Photograph by Helen Blumenschein. Courtesy of State Records Center and Archives. 39711.*

failure and adobe damage, patching of the stucco cracks with cement mortar and repainting. Nestor found the rest of the church to be in generally good condition. He did recommend that this church have a conservator clean and care for the paintings inside. Nestor wrote, "No building is permanent, and an adobe building is less permanent than most. The Mission Churches are certainly worth preserving as part of our religious and cultural past....It seems still possible, when the present coating needs to be replaced, to find economic and social support for a return to mud."[2]

During the next year O'Brien monitored the deteriorating condition of the church, and in early February he asked Archbishop Robert Sanchez to visit and inspect the building. The Archbishop did go to Ranchos de Taos and made some suggestions, such as removing some of the clutter, creating niches for statues and making a small side-chapel in the northeast transept.[3]

Soon thereafter, damp spots were observed on some interior walls along with spalling plaster and peeling paint. A meeting of the Parish Council was called to discuss the rapid deterioration of the walls. Following the meeting, Johnson Nestor was asked to investigate the moisture problem and make recom-

*5:2—A front-end loader helps with the making of the mud plaster in 1979. Photograph by Helen Blumenschein. Courtesy of State Records Center and Archives.*

mendations on how to correct it. Beverly Spears, of that firm, made a thorough investigation of the church and presented a report to Father O'Brien on March 17, 1979, almost a year to the day after the first visit by Robert Nestor. Spears found a large part of the stucco to be in good condition, but it was moderately cracked on the southwest wall of the nave and on the buttresses. The worst cracks she saw were on the buttresses on either side of the front entrance where they were, in some places, over an inch wide and running horizontally across the face of the buttresses so that water flowing down the face would find easy access to the interior. The stucco mesh had broken and was badly rusted. The same type of cracking was noted on the buttresses on the northwest side.

Spears said in her report, "It appears that the cracking of the plaster on the buttresses is caused by the expansion and contracting of the adobe mass beneath the plaster due to moisture. Stucco plaster is permeable to a degree and will permit a small amount of moisture to penetrate. Moisture penetration on a horizontal, or sloped surface, may be enough to cause the adobe beneath to expand and crack the plaster. Freeze/thaw action within the damp plaster may also cause cracks. Once the plaster is cracked, much more moisture penetrates into the adobe, and thus more cracking of the plaster. The moisture also rusts the stucco netting and anchoring nails, which causes further deterioration."

*5:3—When work began in 1979, scaffolding similar to that used in the past was employed. Photograph by Helen Blumenschein. Courtesy of State Records Center and Archives.*

5:4—When a crane was brought to the job, it simplified and speeded up the plastering process. Photograph by Helen Blumenschein. Courtesy of State Records Center and Archives.

5:5—Mostly men are involved in plastering the southwest wall of the church, a departure from tradition. Photograph by Helen Blumenschein 1979. Courtesy of State Records Center and Archives.

Spears also noted that there were wall-high cracks on the interior of the church which corresponded to the location of the roof canales on the exterior. She felt that thermal expansion within the stucco itself caused some of the separations since they seemed worse on the south-facing walls. She noted, however, that the general condition of the church was "very sound."

Spears offered four alternatives: first, repair the existing stucco, after sandblasting to remove the paint (pointing out that this was a temporary solution at best); second, strip and repair the front buttresses and patch cracks elsewhere; third, strip and mud plaster the front facade only, thus postponing the removal of all the stucco until more funds could be found; and fourth, remove all the stucco, repair the walls and replaster with mud. Assuming the work would be done by a contractor, she estimated the costs to run from $3,600 for the second alternative to $41,000 for removing the stucco and mud plastering the entire church.

The architect obviously favored replastering with mud and made a strong appeal saying, "Current sentiment in architectural preservation favors using mud plaster on adobe buildings which were originally mud plastered because it is historically accurate and because mud plaster is more compatible with adobe construction than stucco, both aesthetically and in regard to adherance, thermal expansion, etc. But the cost of its upkeep and a feeling that there are newer, better materials has usually ruled out its use."[4]

In the summer of 1979 the Council authorized the installation of a new roof and, at the same time, made an examination of the interior walls. At some places where moisture had been observed they found wet mud behind the surface. On June 25, 1979, architects Nestor and Spears inspected the buttresses on the northwest walls of the sacristy and transepts and the large buttress at the rear of the apse. The adobe beneath the stucco was crumbling and damp. Two small holes dug into the adobe to a depth of 40 inches showed the adobe to have a uniformly high water content. In their field report they said that the stucco was acting to retain the moisture, forcing it to penetrate more deeply into the buttresses. They recommended uncovering the other buttresses, replacing the bad adobe and covering it back with galvanized stucco mesh and cement plaster (stucco) as a temporary solution. They said that the 12-year experiment with the cement stucco was not a good solution since, when it cracks, it hides the water damage to the adobe beneath and accelerates the damage by retaining the moisture within the walls. They urged the parish to return to mud plaster when it was able.[5]

On July 3 Leo J. V. Gonzales, president of the Parish Council, wrote Archbishop Sanchez apprising him of the situation at the church and asking for assistance. He said the work on the buttresses had started but the church had very limited funds and would welcome any help the archbishop could give.[6]

Father O'Brien wrote the archbishop on the ninth, sending him the architects' reports and pointing out that the church had used all of its funds on the repairs and remodeling, not realizing the serious deterioration of the buttresses. He asked for not only financial help but also prayer and moral support.[7]

*5:6—The 1990 replastering followed the same process as in recent years. The straw bales and the adobe dirt are piled beside the mixing box. Photograph by the author.*

Archbishop Sanchez replied very positively to their requests and said he would immediately seek funds for the work.[8]

In early August the workers pulled back some of the stucco on the southwest side of the church and found the adobe damp but not weak. The stucco was removed from the spherical buttress on the northeast side next to the rectory and it was muddy, partially hollow and in very bad condition. At that point the church leaders decided to return entirely to mud plaster but to leave the concrete block parapets. The block would be covered with wire mesh and plastered with mud. The intention was to work on the church piece by piece continuously until completed.[9]

There was a feeling among the members of the Council that, if asked, the members of the parish would help get the repairs done. In order to get the work started Mario Barela, a mayordomo of Ranchos de Taos, told Father O'Brien to go down the parish list of families and call the people to work on a certain day or provide food for the workers. The 600 families in the parish were divided into groups of 25 and each group was assigned days to come and work.[10]

The first weeks were taken up with the making of adobe brick. Mayordomo Eduardo Duran provided some space in the yard of his home. The parishioners made about 40,000 adobes in the traditional way and stacked them in the sun to dry. It was not long before mechanical help in the form of backhoes and front-end loaders was volunteered and the work went much faster. As the stacks grew beyond the capacity of Duran's yard the work was moved to the rear yard of the rectory where another 20,000 or so bricks were made.

The buttresses were found to be in such bad shape it was decided to remove them entirely and rebuild them as much like the existing ones as possible. Before the buttresses were removed a contractor warned Father Mike that without them the church would collapse. A fellow priest who visited the site also warned him that removing the buttresses all at one time would be a mistake, so there is little wonder that Father Mike

*5:7—The crane hoists the plasterers to the top of the wall to work on the parapet. Photograph by the author. 1990.*

5:8—The woman wearing the bonnet, Eloisa (Loy) Mondragon, is smoothing the final coat. She has been an "enjarradora" many times before. Photograph by the author. 1990.

5:9—Water is being sprayed on the buttress and the plaster is being smoothed prior to receiving the final coat. The part of the buttress in the foreground has already received the finish coat. Photograph by the author. 1990.

had a nightmare about it. His bedroom in the rectory was just across the narrow little street from the northeast arm of the transept of the church where there is a fairly large buttress. He dreamed one night that the buttresses were removed and the church did collapse upon him. In reality, though, the buttresses were not all removed at one time and there was no structural damage. Reinforced concrete foundations were constructed and some 5,000 adobes were used to rebuild the northeast and southwest buttresses; 10,000 were needed to rebuild the large one on the northwest behind the sanctuary.[11]

One day, while I was at the church, Father O'Brien showed me a box full of bones, some of them quite large leg bones, that had been found in the buttresses. He asked me if I could find out what kind of bones they were, so I took them to the Anthropology Department at the University of New Mexico where various faculty members examined them. They proved to be mostly from domestic animals, cattle, sheep, hogs, but also there were bones of deer and elk. No one I have talked with about this has any idea why they were put in the buttresses.

Even though the cement stucco was cracked in many places, it proved very difficult to remove from the church walls. It was thick and tough and the wire lath was well anchored. The workers used pickaxes, hammers and sledges to break it up. Then the steel wire mesh had to be cut and the pieces broken into small enough sections to be carried away by hand. Eventually a pneumatic drill came to the rescue and broke the material away from the walls. A construction hoist was used in place of the ladders for work on the high walls.

It was also found that the entire wall around the churchyard was in bad condition and had to be rebuilt. The wall was found to be so wet that an earthworm, christened "Herman" by Father Mike, was living comfortably inside it.[12]

After the walls and buttresses were repaired and rebuilt, the older members of the parish instructed the younger people in the art of mud plastering. As I have described, in the early days the plastering was done by the women of the parish, but this time many men were

5:10— *The crane was in use again in 1993. Photograph by the author. 1993.*

involved in the effort. The men had always provided the plaster, with the eldest sifting the clay, the middle-aged group mixing it with the straw and water and the younger ones taking it to the women plasterers. This time the backhoe and front-end loader helped with the mixing of the plaster as they had with the adobe making. A wooden scaffold, like the old-fashioned ones, was used in the beginning to support the plasterers, but before long a crane was brought to the job site and used as is shown in Photograph 5:7. However, when the finishing time came in 1979, the grandmother of one of the "enjarradoras" had to be called in to show them how to do the finish coat.[13]

The plaster was applied up to the roof line and stopped there in late October because cold weather was approaching and there was indecision about what to do with the concrete block parapets installed in 1967. It was finally decided to leave the block in place, cover it with stucco mesh and mud plaster it in the spring.

5:11—*Modern steel scaffolding has been erected against the wall next to the sacristy. Photograph by the author. 1993.*

5:12—1993 the northeast wall of the churchyard was demolished and reconstructed using concrete block. It was coated with mud plaster. Photograph by the author.

5:13—After an "encuentro" with women from other northern New Mexico churches, Father Johnny Lee Chavez followed by the Penitente Brothers and others leads them into the plaza. They have come to Ranchos de Taos to bring greetings and good wishes to Saint Francis of Assisi church. Photograph by the author. 1993.

While the work was going on, those members of the parish who were to furnish food for the workers were contacted by the mayordomo in charge who told each of them what to prepare every day. The meals were served to the workers at noon from the kitchen of the rectory and they ate in the back yard. The food was very good and the workers looked forward to having a feast every noon after having had coffee and doughnuts at mid-morning. In the middle of the afternoon they were served soft drinks and cookies, and after work there was beer.[14]

The work lasted for 14 weeks until halted by the approaching cold. Archbishop Sanchez sent the parish a letter of congratulation on their choices, and on Saturday, September 29, he paid a surprise visit, joining Father O'Brien and the mayordomos in a farewell banquet for the mayordomos who had finished their annual term and their newly appointed successors. On Wednesday, October 3, at evening vespers Father Conrad (probably Conrad Runnebaum, a former Franciscan priest from Arroyo Seco) gave the sermon, which was appropriate since the Franciscan Fray Pereyro had built the church. A Fiesta Mass was celebrated on October 4 honoring the patron saint, St. Francis of Assisi. After the procession following the Mass, the outgoing mayordomos turned over their responsibility for the church to their successors. During the singing of the "entriega" the statue of Saint Francis was given to the new mayordomos along with medallions signifying their office. During the offertory two elderly members of the parish were joined by two children symbolizing the work done by people of all ages.[15] The following Sunday, after mass, a fiesta was held in the gymnasium honoring all who had participated in the work. There was lots of good food, drinks and dancing to a group of local musicians playing traditional melodies.

As soon as the weather permitted, in the spring of 1980, the parishioners began reworking the parapets and the rest of the walls. The application of the mud plaster over the concrete block parapets seems to have worked well. The work was finished by August 15,

1980, in time for the Feast of the Assumption of the Blessed Virgin. At the Mass Father Mike led the procession around the church, celebrating a job well done.

All of the work was done by mayordomo Eduardo Duran, who acted as foreman, with four paid helpers and dozens of members of the parish: the elders, men, women, teenagers and children. They did it with no outside help, other than what was offered voluntarily, and returned the church to its original appearance. Soon after the work was completed, word was received that some of the walls of San Juan Nepomuceno Church at El Rito had collapsed because of a drainage problem and would have to be rebuilt. Consequently, the 5,000 unused adobe bricks that were made for St. Francis church were given to the El Rito church.[16]

*5:14—The winter of 1993 was hard on the mud plaster as evidenced by the deterioration taking place on the southwest walls. This picture was taken on June 7, 1994, while the annual replastering of the church was under way. Photograph by the author.*

In an article in the *Sangre de Cristo Chronicle* on October 11, 1979, Father O'Brien was asked about what would happen to the church in the future. Would the people continue the tradition of replastering with mud, or should the parish try to find federal funds since it was such an architectural masterpiece? Father O'Brien replied, "It is a living church and the first priority must be prayer. The worst thing that could happen to it would be to become a museum." He believed any use of federal funds would compromise the very meaning of what the Spanish settlers of 1710 began. He continued, "If the people don't want to love the church any more, it should go back to the earth."[17]

Since 1980 the church has been replastered with mud every summer by the parishioners. Photographs 5:6 through 5:12 show the work being done in July, 1990, and 1993. The parishioners were divided into eleven groups of 84 people, in alphabetical order, and one clean-up crew of 38 to work on the last day. As in past years they gave of their labor, their money, their material or their food. When I visited the site in 1990 there were about 15 men and women working at replastering. The whole job was completed in two six-day work weeks. In 1992, the northeast wall of the churchyard was rebuilt using concrete block, but plastered with mud.

*5:15—The street on the northeast side was closed and a crane placed to hoist plasterers to work on the tower. June 7, 1994. Photograph by the author.*

## CHAPTER 6—RESTORATION OF THE ALTAR SCREENS AND PAINTINGS, 1980–81

An early inventory of Saint Francis of Assisi church was made in 1817–1818 for the visitor Guevara. The ornaments were few and briefly noted:

"One altar screen with an image of the Lord of Esquipulas,

"The high altar with two figures in the round,

"One altar screen dedicated to the Patriarch St. Joseph,

and an image of the Holy Patriarch."

Both the main altar screen and that of Esquipulas in the northeast arm of the transept are still in place today. The latter screen has over 400 square feet of surface. It has eight panels in three tiers and at the top are three Franciscan emblems. The two large bultos in the side altar are of Our Lady of Sorrows and the Blessed Ludovina, or Lydwina, of Holland. This side altar is shown in Photograph 6:1 and in the HABS watercolor drawing on sheet 32. The main, or high altar, has eight paintings on canvas and a statue of St. Francis in a niche in the lower tier. The main altar screen is depicted in Photographs 6:2 and 6:3. The HABS drawings 15, 16 and 32 show details of the screens. All of these pieces were donated by various people and the altars and screens were constructed on the site as described in Chapter Two.[1]

In a 1953 article about the cleaning of the paintings and altar screens, the Spanish colonial arts historian E. Boyd wrote, "The reredos (of the altar in the transept) is in the style of Molleno, a prolific and highly individualistic 'santero,' whose known dated pieces fall between 1829 and 1845. (When she wrote *Popular Arts of Spanish New Mexico* in 1974 she used an earlier date, 1804, as the start of his work.) The composition is unusually formal compared to some 'santero' altarpieces in that the figures are separated by painted swags, wooden moldings and twisted pillars. The three tiers of panels contain eight figures with a central alcove at the bottom housing fine 'bultos'." It was her opinion, based on observation of the surface treatment and brushwork of the paintings and the bultos, that they were painted, and possibly carved, by the same santero.[2]

Father Pereyro, as missionary at Laguna and Acoma between 1798 and 1803, may have known Molleno or have become familiar with his work. Pereyro was very active in making improvements and alterations to the churches where he was located and may even have been the "Laguna santero" as suggested by W. E. Stallings, Jr., a dendrochronologist. To Boyd it was clear that the santero paintings at Ranchos were not done by the same person who did the work at Laguna. Molleno was probably a student of the Laguna artist.

There is no documentary evidence in the form of a birth record or of business

*6:1—The reredos in the right, northeast transept. 1934. HABS Collection, Prints and Photographic Division, Library of Congress.*

*6:2—The main altar and the lower part of the reredos in 1934. HABS Collection, Prints and Photographic Division, Library of Congress.*

transactions to identify Molleno, who today remains a shadowy figure. His name was found on the back of one panel so that he has been recognized as the artist formerly known as the "chile painter" because many of his panels contain red space fillers that suggest ripe chile peppers. While working in Ranchos de Taos, Molleno must have made many contacts since he subsequently did work at Talpa, Trampas, Chimayo, Taos and other places in northern New Mexico.

There has been much speculation about what happened to the altar and screen of the Patriarch St. Joseph that vanished from the southwest transept. When E. Boyd was working in Ranchos de Taos in 1953, a former sacristan said that they had been bought by a rich American some thirty years before. She speculated that they might have been the work of Molleno and they may have been composed of the eight unassembled panels now in the collection of the Denver Art Museum.[3]

Sometime in the last quarter of the nineteenth century the crucifix of Esquipulas was partially overpainted and the altar screen in the northeast transept was whitewashed over except for the niche and the statues in it . This was mentioned by Governor L. Bradford Prince who wrote in his book, *Spanish Mission Churches of New Mexico,* in 1915, "The altar is comparatively new, in the modern French style, but the reredos behind the altar has not been modernized and apparently has remained unchanged from the time of the building of the church. It includes eight pictures of saints painted on canvas. On the north side (referring to the altar screen in the northeast transept) is another reredos containing eight pictures of saints painted on wood and of New Mexican workmanship. These, as well as some others on the south side (possibly meaning the St. Joseph altar screen), have been whitewashed over the paintings at some remote period, and the marks of that covering are not yet entirely removed."[4]

In 1929 the whitewash was still only partially removed, but a guide book to the state published in 1940 said, "The large reredos, 25 feet high with its carved pillars and wooden partitions, contains seven paintings so old that it is impossible to tell which saints most of them represent. There are several old paintings done on wood by native artists."[5] Maybe the writer miscounted the number of paintings, but obviously they were heavily covered with dirt and smoke. There had been coal and/or wood burning stoves in the church for many years which surely contributed to the problem.

Father Paul Hatch initiated a project to clean and restore the paintings and statues in 1953. The project was sponsored by Museum of New Mexico Director Boaz Long, who took the view that the functions of the institution were state-wide and that preservation of regional landmarks was vital to the future of the state. Hatch hired Taos artist Bert Phillips to clean the paintings on the main altar. He was advised and assisted by E. Boyd, who was at that time associate and curator in the Museum's Department of Spanish Colonial Art, and Elmer Shupe, a well-known resident of Taos, who volunteered his services.

*6:3—The main altar and screen as it was in February, 1994. Photograph by John Martin Campbell.*

Boyd wrote in December, 1953, "The height of the reredos required a scaffolding, which was provided by Father Hatch. The paintings and the superimposed whitewash being equally water soluable, it was necessary to experiment with solvents which should not injure the pigments of 'yeso' ground. Several were tested and naptha was found to be the most satisfactory, despite its volatility and detrimental effect on human lungs. After the whitewash was removed, the surfaces were sponged with pure turpentine and a film of hot liquid wax was applied to protect the paintings from temperature and humidity variations almost indefinitely."

She continued, "The Ranchos construction consisted of narrow strips of boards, loosely fitted so that the original surfaces were covered with the gypsum plaster over each edge; and later shifting of the planks did not injure the paintings. The thinness of the 'yeso' ground has also contributed to the preservation of the total surface since it has not flaked off from inherent deterioration, but is lost only where it has been scrubbed away by human agency."[6] She later wrote that it took five days to remove the remaining whitewash from the altar screen in the northeast transept, that the lower panels had been eroded by cleaning with wet rags and that above the level that could be reached from the floor, the paint was in good condition as was the yeso, or gesso, ground.[7]

In appreciation of the Museum's help, Father Hatch made a gift to the Spanish Colonial Arts Department of a retable panel, done in the style of Molleno around 1820. It had not been in Ranchos church for many years. It was on a hand-hewn plank, five feet wide and twenty inches high, with crossbones of geometric design and three skulls under a row of swags. The skulls may have had reference to St. Francis since the santeros sometimes showed him holding a skull. [8] If the panel had been in the church how was it used?

As a part of the total restoration of St. Francis of Assisi church in 1979–80, it was decided to restore the two altar screens. The several paintings in the church had been cleaned by Dina Brovarone, a professional conservator, a couple of years before the restoration of the church began in 1979.

The question about the altar screens was: restore them to what state? The altar screens had been reworked in 1953, but only to preserve what was the existing condition at that time. Nothing more had been done until Father Michael O'Brien discussed with the parish council a suitable way to celebrate St. Francis's 800th anniversary. They authorized the restoration of the screens and agreed to assess each family $25 and to raise additional funds for a total budget of $20,000.[9]

They employed Luis Tapia, a young man recognized for his traditional and contemporary styles of carving, and Fred Vigil, an artist from Santa Fe. With Father O'Brien they visited several churches where the Laguna santero was believed to have worked, including Acoma, Zia and Laguna pueblos and San Miguel church in Santa Fe. They concluded that the same artist was responsible for the main altar screen at St. Francis. They agreed that the altar screen in the northeast transept was the work of Molleno, his pupil.

*6:4—View of the main altar and retable from the nave. February, 1994. Photograph by John Martin Campbell.*

When the restorers began their work they found the original water-base paint colors faded with age and obscured by varnish that had darkened with time. Removing the liquid wax which was applied in 1953 was quite a chore and it was discovered that the wax had been more destructive than the varnish.

The old colors, when uncovered and dampened, showed how they must have looked originally. The restorers matched them as closely as possible with modern water-base paints. Then they covered the screens with a polymer coat for protection. They also repaired broken and rotten pieces of the wood, both on the front and back. No damage to the main altar from the moisture that had penetrated the buttress behind it was found.

One of the more interesting things discovered during the restoration was that under several coats of brown paint and varnish, the robe of the statue of Saint Francis was first painted a deep blue representing the color of the robes worn by some of the Franciscan missionaries in earlier years.[10]

The idea of bringing back the original paint colors did not meet with unanimous approval by any means. Art lovers and art historians appealed to the parish council to merely clean the altar screens and recoat them with a protective finish. Some people felt that the paints used were too garish, but Father O'Brien, looking back on the decision, felt it was the right thing to do.

The 800th anniversary of Saint Francis was celebrated at a vesper service on Saturday, October 3, 1981. During the procession, while the statue of the saint was taken out of the church, the curtain hiding the tall screen behind the main altar was removed, revealing the reredo in authentic recreation of its original colors: deep red, bright green, black and white. Archbishop Robert Sanchez rededicated the church during the ceremony.[11]

## CHAPTER 7—THE HISTORIC AMERICAN BUILDINGS SURVEY IN TAOS COUNTY
## ST. FRANCIS OF ASSISI CHURCH
## THE CHAPEL OF OUR LADY OF TALPA

This chapter and the accompanying drawings have been included in the book because of the historic importance of the drawings and the making of them. The Historic American Buildings Survey (HABS) was the first nationwide attempt to document historic buildings, and out of those chosen to be done in New Mexico two were in Taos County. St. Francis of Assisi church has survived and is in good condition today. The Chapel of Our Lady of Talpa was not so fortunate and is now in total ruin. It was measured and photographed and drawings were made so the beautiful little chapel is not forgotten.

The Chapel of Our Lady of Talpa, known locally as the Durán Chapel, is also included in this document because the squad leader of the surveyors, Alan Fisher, an architect from Denver, gave us much information about the experiences of the surveyors while they worked in the Taos area. Fisher gave a talk to a group in Denver many years ago and his notes tell much about the impact

*7:1—The Chapel of Our Lady of Talpa seen from across the churchyard. 1934. James Slack photographer. HABS Collection, Prints and Photographic Division, Library of Congress.*

*7:2—Front facade of the Chapel of Our Lady of Talpa, March 15, 1934. Photograph by James Slack, HABS Collection, Prints and Photographs Division, Library of Congress.*

New Mexico had on these young men, and what life in Taos was like in 1934. Unfortunately, none of the crew that measured St. Francis church left such a record for posterity.

The chapel was built in 1838 by Nicholás Sandoval on a site next to his house in Rio Chiquito. Later, through marriages, the Durán family became the caretakers of it. Leandro Durán was the owner from the early 1900's until his death in 1950.[1] Photographs 7:4 and 7:5, which I took in the summer of 1991, show some of the walls are still standing, but it is mostly just a pile of earth overgrown with weeds. Great efforts were made in the 1940's to save the chapel from ruin by many well known Taos people, including Father José Garcia, who formed the "Durán Chapel Committee." Their efforts came to naught and the altarscreen, bultos and other furnishings were sold.[2]

There is an excellent book titled *The Chapel of Our Lady of Talpa*, by William Wroth, published by the Taylor Museum of the Colorado Springs Fine Arts Center in 1979. Wroth gives a history of the chapel and the surrounding area, a detailed description of the altar screen and a catalog of all the bultos that were purchased for the Taylor Museum in the 1940's.

The Historic American Buildings Survey was a program developed by the National Parks Service (NPS) as a relief project unter the Civil Works Administration (CWA) in the Depression year of 1933. Charles E. Peterson, a young architect with NPS, had been brought to Washington from San Francisco to be chief of the Eastern Division Branch of Plans and Designs and to work on the

Colonial Parkway in Virginia. He was only 26 years of age, but he was deeply concerned about the less fortunate architects and draftsmen who were unemployed and who could see no opportunities for work . Peterson also was aware of the continuing loss of undocumented historic structures.[3]

Conservation efforts of the federal government's New Deal were concentrated in the Civilian Conservation Corps, but private funds were being used to restore colonial Williamsburg. On November 13, 1933, Peterson sent a memorandum to NPS Director Arno Cammerer introducing his proposal for "Relief employment under CWA of Architectural Profession in program recording interesting and significant specimens of American Architecture." He urged, "If the great number of buildings must disappear through economic causes, they should not pass into unrecorded oblivion." He also said, "...the chief virtues of this plan are that men could go to work (preparing a collection of measured drawings augmented by photographs and other data) almost at once and that an enormous contribution to the history and aesthetics of American life could be made."

In this memo, Peterson discussed the need for the program, how the program could be administered, what it would cost and how the data could be collected. Under a section on style of architecture he stated, "Special attention would be given to the early work of New Orleans and Santa Fe."  In another paragraph he wrote, "Exact records should be made of such constructions as the Taos and Acoma pueblos, and the Zuni villages farther West where mutations are fast encroaching upon the flavor of the native aboriginal style. Recording of some of the highly perishable prehistoric remains such as Pueblo Bonita (sic), New Mexico, should be included." Peterson said far more about New Mexico buildings than about those in any other state.[4]

The proposal received immediate enthusiastic reception from the Secretary of the Interior, Harold L. Ickes, who approved it on November 17, 1933. The Federal Relief Administration approved it on December 1. The appointment of facilitating personnel in Washington and the field was immediately begun.

The country was divided into 39 districts with a district officer in each nominated by the American Institute of Architects (AIA) and appointed by the Secretary of the Interior. An arrangement had been reached with the AIA to have it help with the administration of the work. The newly appointed officers were to contact the local CWA officers to secure architects and draftsmen for the field parties. Office space had to be obtained gratis from public institutions or private citizens.[5]

 Peterson recommended John Gaw Meem, the well known Santa Fe architect, to be one of the four architects to serve on the National Advisory Committee. Meem immediately accepted, stating in his letter to Peterson that it had been his own dream to do such a survey.[6]

John Gaw Meem was made district officer for the district consisting of New Mexico, Arizona and part of Utah by the president of the Colorado Chapter of the AIA which was composed of Colorado, New Mexico and Wyoming.[7] He accepted, but he soon turned the position over to Leicester Hyde, an architect with NPS in Santa Fe. The Laboratory of Anthropology in Santa Fe offered space for the district office.[8]

Since there were only a handful of architectural firms in New Mexico and very few draftsmen, finding unemployed people competent to do the work turned out to be impossible. While he was acting as the district officer Meem had received notice from Thomas C. Vint, chief architect of the National Park Service, that the quota of men for his district was thirteen. Meem immediately wired back saying he could use a hundred men and asked if he could recruit from other states with more unemployed people.[9] Vint told him he could use men from Colorado[10] and from that state, and almost entirely from Denver, came most of the architects and draftsmen who worked on the HABS projects in New Mexico. There were probably letters and printed notices sent around recruiting people, but most of those employed learned of the project by word of mouth. A total of thirty-two men were employed during the course of the work, based on the names on the drawings. I have not found any roster of the employees.

Only one of the men who came to New Mexico, Bradley Paige Kidder from Denver, remained in New Mexico after the HABS work was completed. He worked in Meem's office until World War II and after serving in the Navy began his own architectural practice. In 1958 he became a partner in the firm of McHugh and Hooker, Bradley P. Kidder and Associates. Kidder was one of the first architects in the state to be made a fellow in the AIA and one of the very few architects in the country to receive the coveted Kemper Award for service to the Institute.

The rules established by the Washington office required that the people employed must be chosen for their ability from those listed on the rolls of the unemployed at the nearest Federal Reemployment Office. They were to be organized into squads of two to eight men depending on the size of the project and the economy of transportation. The ranking member was called the squad leader and was responsible to the district officer. The squad leader was paid $1.10 per hour and the other squad members received ninety cents an hour. They were limited to thirty hours work per week. Each man had to furnish his own drawing board, T-square, scales and all other drawing equipment except paper, pencils and erasers, which were supplied by HABS. HABS also provided surveying equipment such as levels and rods. If the work was done in the city where they lived they received no travel reimbursement, but if it was out of town they had to use a privately owned car and they got four cents a mile plus $2.50 per day subsistence.[11]

Because of Meem's long-standing interest in measuring and recording historic buildings he was most anxious to compile a list of proposed structures to be surveyed. On December 26, 1933, he sent a six-page list of projects to Hyde "which I have had in mind since the American Historic Building Survey (sic) first came to my attention." Meem's understanding was that only buildings which had remained unaltered and those in a state of disrepair were eligible for the survey.[12] This first list was followed by a more comprehensive list, probably compiled in cooperation with Hyde and others, which was sent to Vint on January 5, 1934, unsigned. St. Francis of Assisi Church was included in the first list and in all subsequent lists. In the list sent to Hyde Meem referred to it as the 'Old Church, Ranchos de Taos' and said, "Should be measured in detail. The district around Ranchos de Taos contains some very fine specimens of Spanish-pueblo architecture and should be included in a careful survey." In the later list of projects sent to Vint the church is called the 'Mission of Los Ranchos de Taos.' The accompanying statement said, "One of the finest of the early New Mexico missions erected near Taos, N. M. Still used. This church should by all means be measured as it remains essentially as it was built. 3 sheets."

The Chapel of Our Lady of Talpa only appeared on the final list. The description said, "An exquisite little chapel near Taos that is in fine condition. Probably erected prior to 1820." Because of the limitations of time, money and personnel the list of buildings to be measured in 1934 was reduced to ten, of which St. Francis was number seven and the Talpa chapel was number ten.[13]

Applications for employment began to arrive in Santa Fe in early December. On January 2, 1934, the first day work in the field was authorized, a squad went to work measuring San Miguel Church in Santa Fe.[14]

Victor Hornbein, later to become a distinguished Denver architect, was one of the HABS surveyors. He wrote in a recent letter, "We were all architects, architectural draftsmen or architectural students and we all had a suitable background. We were all very much aware of the aims of HABS over and above the underlying reason for the project, that of providing paid work for a profession that was totally disrupted by the depression. I think all of us knew that the United States was probably alone amongst the great nations in having virtually no records of buildings with historic or aesthetic value, and, although the opportunity for earning thirty dollars a week for thirty hours of time was, in most cases, an overriding reason, participation in the recording of these buildings was of great importance to us. For both reasons most of us were disappointed when the funds ran out leaving so very many buildings unrecorded."

Hornbein said he did not remember any formal organizational meetings. The team agreed among themselves with a minimum of discussion how they would go about the work. They had all had experience in measuring buildings for alterations, and they had usually had to prepare construction drawings after they had completed the measurements. Hornbein said, "it (the measuring of buildings for remodeling) was much easier." None of them had had the experience of measuring an adobe building. He said the oft repeated joke after each infrequent rain storm was that they would have to start all over. [15]

The field party, or squad, assigned to measure St. Francis arrived in Ranchos de Taos on February 5, 1934, and immediately began work. They worked on the site obtaining data until around March 8. The squad leader was Benjamin J. Blosser from Los Angeles, California, and the field party consisted of John J. Thompson, William P. Cover, Karl Mertz and R. G. McComas. In order to establish a base line for measuring the irregular layout of St. Francis Church, an axis was established down the center of the church from the centerline of the front doors to the center of the opening into the sanctuary. From that point another axis was drawn to the center of the rear wall of the sanctuary. Off of the centerline they turned a right angle from the south corner of the southwest arm of the transept and made this intersection the control point for the lateral measurements and set it as the benchmark of 0'-0" for all vertical measurements, which were made using a surveyor's level furnished by HABS. Off of these axes a grid was established both inside and outside the church, even on the roof. Stakes were driven and lines were strung outside the building while inside chalk marks were made on the floor. From these grid lines measurements were taken of the inside and outside faces of the walls and recorded in their notebook. The dimensions were taken at the level of the floor inside and at grade level outside the building. A similar measuring technique was used for the Talpa Chapel.

The vertical dimensions, both inside and outside, were obtained by dropping tapes from ladders placed against the walls and from the roof. The surveyor's level was used to measure the differences in elevation of the floor, the roof and the grade around the perimeter of the building. The men used white butcher paper and brown wrapping paper, torn, not cut, to make rubbings of certain features such as the corbels, the carvings on the braces beneath the beams and the newel post of the stair to the choir loft. (Rubbings are made by placing a piece of paper over the object to be copied and, using a soft pencil, going back and forth over the paper until an image of the object beneath is produced.) From these rubbings they made their drawings of the details they wanted to record.

*Illustration 7:1—Field notes made by the HABS surveyors of the measurements of the roof over the transept and sanctuary of the Ranchos de Taos church. From these notes that part of the roof plan on Sheet 7 of the HABS drawing was done. This is typical of the notes made for all parts of the building. Reproduced from the HABS Collection, Prints and Photographic Division, Library of Congress.*

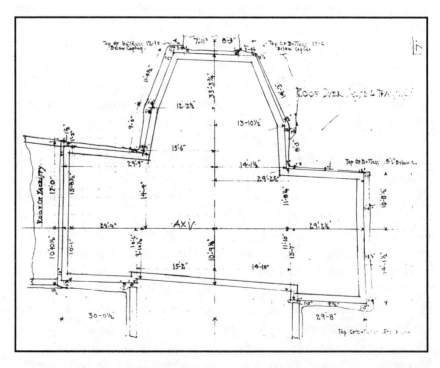

Since most of the teams were small, it was necessary for the entire team to do the measuring which had to be almost complete before any drawing could start.[16]

The men did the drawings in their rooms after making the field measurements. Work on the Ranchos drawings began on March 8 and was completed on April 8. At Talpa measuring went from March 8 to March 22 and the drawing took from March 23 to April 5, 1934, according to the dates on the drawings.[17] Each member of the party produced some drawings individually and some were worked on by two people. William Cover drew Sheet 32 of the Ranchos de Taos set in color and Alan Fisher did Sheet 12 of the Talpa set in color. Both are elevations of altar screens. The other sheets were done in India ink on heavy vellum paper. Hornbein, reminiscing about his experiences as a HABS worker, wrote that he did not think there was any particular pattern in the assignment of the drawings. He supposed that the older, more experienced men took over the plan and section sheets, leaving elevations and details to the younger squad members, but this was not necessarily typical of all HABS projects. Generally, the better draftsmen were given the more important sheets to do. He said that since drawing style, like handwriting, is unique they tried to achieve a certain uniformity by defining line weights and conventions, but each man's work is recognizable.

Hornbein noted that much of the final drawing was done free-hand without the help of a T-square and triangle. This was because there were not very many straight lines in the adobe structure, making the drawings even more individualistic. He and Stanley Kent spent the month of June in Santa Fe working at the Laboratory of Anthropology doing the cover sheets for all of the HABS projects. After they finished that work they drove over to Acoma to join the other survey-

*7:3—This photograph is titled "The Forbidden Church, Talpa," and was probably made in the 1950's. It shows the chapel in an advanced state of decay. Center for Southwest Research, General Library,University of New Mexico. 000-479-0263.*

*7:4—Looking across the churchyard, 1991. Photograph by the author.*

ors. "Stan Kent and I stayed on until the last line was inked in mid-August, as I remember, and left New Mexico to take up again what we thought of as the dull, uneventful life we had led before the enchantment of New Mexico."[18]

The HABS program was to begin winding down in February, 1934, with the remaining work to be completed as soon as possible. In New Mexico the biggest job was the measuring and drawing of Acoma Pueblo, so as teams finished the smaller projects many of them were transferred to Acoma, but many decided to leave New Mexico. A total of twenty-one men worked at Acoma, but none of the members of the Ranchos de Taos squad went to Acoma or worked on any other of the ten buildings completed in 1934, according to the list of team members shown on the drawings.[19] Hornbein wrote that work on the drawings continued until late May or early June, but the Acoma project lasted until August after additional funds were allocated.

It certainly was not all work and no play for the young men on the team. After only thirty hours' work each week, there was plenty of leisure time. Hornbein reminisced about joining Alan Fisher and Paul Atchison, both also from Denver, in the bar at La Fonda in Santa Fe on a beautiful June afternoon while Atchison discussed at great lengths the merits of Martell's cognac over that of Hennessey.[20]

Fisher was a member of the squad that measured "La Capilla de Nuestra Señora de Talpa." He told of his experiences in a talk he gave in Denver many years ago. Fisher was the squad leader of the team that consisted of Bradley Kidder, H. P. Atchison, A. B. Willison and Art Hoyer. He described it as a "movable feast," "... an experience of younger days, that remains with you in memory where ever you go for the rest of your life."

Fisher talked about the team's arrival in Talpa: "As the CWA recording party entered the Plaza in Bradley Kidder's 1927 Dodge 'Victory' sedan, a feeling of displaced dissolution pervaded the group. The new strangeness of an old world led to loneliness and deep apprehension. This uncomfortable and serious psychological situation eased somewhat in a matter of fifty-seven minutes.

"Within the first hour, the tattered occupants of the Dodge were as well adjusted socially and physically to the new environment as is the bearded artist complacently sitting at a marbletop table at Cafe des Deux Magots pres de St. Michel. Thus we set the table for the 'Movable Feast'."

Fisher and his group stayed at Captain O'Hay's cottage camp in Taos for awhile until they were offered accommodations by Ruth Swaine at her Talpa ranch, "La Cumbre." Through her they met many of the famous and near famous citizens of 1934 Taos including Victor Higgins, Mabel Dodge Luhan, Ward Lockwood, Spud Johnson, Mike Cunico and many others. Rebecca Strand, later known as Rebecca James, a close friend of Georgia O'Keeffe, lived at the Harwood Foundation House where she painted flowers on glass. She, whom Fisher described as "...warm, thoughtful, colorful beyond ability to describe," showed him the Martinez House "...in great understanding." One of the local characters who impressed him was Bing Abbott whom he called "a real good friend, he was sort of philosopher-carpenter-builder as such and seemed to have the valley's construction problems well in hand." Fisher recounted the famous Manby case which was on everyone's mind. Arthur

*7:5—Crumbling ruins are all that are left of the chapel, 1991. Photograph by the author.*

Manby was a local character who had presumably been murdered but his head was missing. Fisher talked about John Dunn, a great "sage" and gambler of the time who also drove a Model T Ford taxi back and forth to Taos Junction to met the Chili Line trains. For Fisher, the Talpa squad, and I'm sure for the Ranchos de Taos party also, it was truly a "movable feast."

After the work was completed, Fisher was left behind at La Cumbre for a few days to make the watercolor rendering of the chapel reredos. He finished it in the morning and left, returning in the afternoon to pick up the brushes and palette only to find that three-year old Hailiea Duran had eaten all the watercolor paints.[21]

The HABS drawings, field notes and eleven photographs of St. Francis of Assisi Church, as well as the material on Our Lady of Talpa Chapel with six photographs, are all housed in the Library of Congress. There is similar documentation of over 20,000 other historic structures. It is estimated that over thirty percent of the buildings surveyed in 1934 have subsequently been destroyed. "La Capilla de Señora de Talpa," as it is titled on the drawings, is one of those that has returned to the earth from which it was made so many years ago, but it did not go unrecorded into oblivion. When restoration work was done on the Ranchos de Taos church in the 1960's and 1970's, the HABS drawings were invaluable to the architects.

On June 28, 1990, I visited the Library of Congress primarily to look at the field notes made by the 1934 HABS squad that worked on St. Francis. I had hoped there would be more notes than appeared on the drawings, but there were not. Still, it was a great pleasure to feast my eyes on the beautiful original drawings and think what a wonderful experience it must have been for those young men from other states to live and work in the Ranchos de Taos area—in another world so completely different from theirs.

## CHAPTER 8 — THE MISSIONS OF ST. FRANCIS OF ASSISI CHURCH

Introduction by Corina A. Santistevan

The study of the physical structure of a church is incomplete without considering the inner structure, the community of faith that is responsible from the moment the idea of a church is conceived to its realization and to its continued maintenance. An adobe building is just a building which, if not tended and cared for, will break down and return to the earth from which it arose. It is people who build a church, care for a church and in the end become the church.

The Church of San Francisco de Asís as a parish extends from the lowlands of Talpa on the east to Los Cordovas/Cordillera and lower Ranchitos on the west, from the ridges of Llano Quemado on the south to undefined borders on the north. It is measured more in terms of where the people live who become members of the parish than by any land area or specified border.

The Ranchos de Taos church was built as an "ayuda de parroquia," a mission of the mother church of San Gerónimo de Taos at Taos Pueblo. Although it was much larger than the usual chapel, its purpose as a place of worship was the same as that of its three small mission chapels in use today. The chapel in Talpa is dedicated to Our Lady of St. John of the Lakes; Llano Quemado's chapel is dedicated to Our Lady of Mt. Carmel and the chapel used by the communities of Los Cordovas/Cordillera and lower Ranchitos has St. Isidore as its patron saint. These three chapels are used weekly during Advent and Lent and monthly for vigil mass on Saturday.

Chapels were built by the people of a community, sometimes as private "oratorios," which were not necessarily licensed by the diocese as mission churches used to be in the earlier centuries. However, some of these oratorios or chapels were deeded to the Catholic diocese at different times and now belong to the Archdiocese of Santa Fe. The Ranchos area still has two private oratorios which have remained private or become community property.

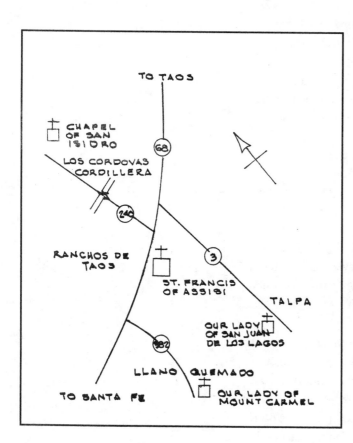

*Illustration 8:1—A location map.*

Michael Miller in *Monuments of Adobe* defines succinctly the purpose for which the Hispanic New Mexican churches, chapels and moradas were built:

> "The iglesias, capillas and moradas which Hispanic New Mexicans built in their frontier communities were smaller versions of the mission churches borrowed from the golden age. They molded them from the earth, to honor a patron saint and to provide places for religious devotion. The people placed great significance on these simple architectural monuments and every village had its chapel, built with great sacrifice and devotion by its inhabitants. These architectural symbols of religious and cultural expression became, in many respects, the center of New Mexico village life."[1]

That is true of today's mission chapels. When the chapel for San Isidro was built in the early 1950's, it served to unify the communities of Cordillera and Los Cordovas; it made individuals aware of their place in the mother church and it created a sense of responsibility for the care of their own chapel and for the church in Ranchos de Taos. The chapels serve as centers for the communities.

*8:1—The chapel of Our Lady of St. John of the Lakes in 1943. Photograph by John Collier. Library of Congress collection.*

The Chapel of Our Lady of Saint John of the Lakes,
*La Capilla de Nuestra Señora de San Juan de Los Lagos*
by Van Dorn Hooker

This sturdily built little chapel sits on the southeast side of a small plaza just to the west of the Las Vegas highway about two miles southeast of Ranchos de Taos. The chapel faces northeast toward the road and is flanked by very old adobe houses. It sits far enough from the highway that it does not attract much attention from the passersby. The adobe colored stucco and natural wood trim blend with the surrounding houses on the small plaza. The chapel has been very well maintained through its century and a half and today looks fresh and clean with a recent coat of plaster.

This area, now known as Talpa, on the banks of the Rio Chiquito, was first settled in the late eighteenth century. It was included in the Cristóbal de la Serna grant which later became the lands of Diego Romero and his heirs.

In 1823 a formal community was established on the Rio Chiquito when a settler of the area, Manuel Lucero, gave a piece of land to the local inhabitants for the purpose of building a plaza. It was 150 varas square and ran "from the Camino Real to the Rio Chiquito." In 1827 there were 30 heads of families in the plaza and on nearby ranches. That year Don Bernardo Durán, in the name of twenty citizens, petitioned Don Antonio José Martinez, the parish priest of Taos, for the right to make their special patroness the Virgin Mary in the title of Our Lady of San Juan, Nuestra Señora de San Juan de Rio Chiquito, for whom they promised to have a celebration once a year.

The names Talpa and Nuestra Señora de San Juan de Las Lagos probably originated in Mexico. In the eighteenth and early nineteenth century trading expeditions went annually to Mexico from the Taos area. Local products were taken to Chihuahua and points south and traded for Mexican and European goods. While there the traders took part in religious festivities and pilgrimages to shrines including the popular Nuestra Señora de San Juan de Los Lagos and Nuestra Señora de Talpa in Jalisco. Upon returning the pilgrims must have told stories about the miraculous shrines which inspired religious observances. Not only were their names incorporated but the saints' images were painted on the altar screens and carved into bultos.

The chapel was built in 1828 by the citizens of the area with the support of Don Bernardo Durán. This is confirmed by an inscription on the chapel's altar screen. The people of Rio Chiquito continued to be parishoners of Saint Francis of Assisi in Ranchos de Taos and all of their important religious functions took place there until July 7, 1833, when the Bishop of Durango, Don Juan Antonio Laureano de Zubiria, licensed the holding of divine offices in their chapel.[2] Thereafter, the feast day mass was observed in Talpa although the faithful had to continue attending masses at Our Lady of Guadalupe in Taos or St. Francis in Ranchos de Taos.

8:2—*When this photograph was made a number of years ago there was a garland of flowers, real or artificial, surrounding the statue of Our Lady of Talpa. Photograph by Shaffer's Studio, Taos. Courtesy of the Museum of New Mexico, negative 48652. No date.*

The nave of the chapel is small, seating about 125 people on 13 rows of pews on both sides of the center aisle. The front parapet is topped with miniature towers on the two corners and a center bell tower which houses one bell. There is a pair of front doors with panels in each of them that form a cross. Two double-hung windows with clear glass pierce the side walls of the nave, giving the interior a bright, cheerful feeling. At the rear of the chapel there is a small sacristy and another room on the northeast side which may have been built later. The chapel probably has a viga-supported roof but a fiber board ceiling covers it. The vigas do not extend through the exterior walls today but may have originally. At some time the exposed ends may have rotted from constant exposure to the weather and been cut off and stuccoed over. Today there are three new-looking metal-lined canales extending through the low parapet on the south side. They are sufficiently long to prevent run-off water from splashing against the wall.

The floor, no doubt originally hard packed earth, is now modern hardwood with a carpet runner down the center aisle. The lighting consists of incandescent lamps in round frosted glass or plastic bowls hung from the ceiling. The interior walls are painted white.

In 1856 efforts were being made to raise funds for the repair of the chapel of "San Juan de Rio Chiquito." By whatever means and under whatever titles, the people of Talpa have cared for the chapel and the exquisite retablo by Molleno and Bernardo Durán for more than a century.[3]

*8:3—The altar screen in 1994. Photograph by John Martin Campbell.*

The altar screen of the chapel is small, 7'-0" wide by 7'-4" high, but is in scale with the proportions of the chapel. It sits on a wood frame which raises it 2'-8" above the floor. The screen is very important since it was the work of the famous santero Molleno, sometimes called the Chile Painter, who dated the piece 1828.

The bulto of the patroness, Our Lady of Saint John of the Lakes, may also have been his work, but recent documentary evidence points to José Rafael Aragón as the more likely sculptor. The bulto is set in an arched niche in the center of the upper part of the screen designed specially to emphasize the statue.

*8:4—The exterior of the Talpa chapel. Photograph by John Martin Campbell, July 28, 1994.*

E. Boyd in *Popular Arts of Spanish New Mexico* notes that Molleno for the first time faced all of the saints in the surrounding panels inward toward the center. She identified them as Santiago in the upper right and San Antonio in the panel below. The lower panel on the left is inscribed, "Mi Sñora de Talpa," a rarely used title for Mary the mother of Jesus. The panel above is titled "San Brnrdo," probably the abbreviation of San Bernardo de Siena, the patron saint of the donor, Don Bernardo Durán.[4] It was the custom at that time to honor benefactors who helped build retables.

## The Chapel of Our lady of Mount Carmel in Llano Quemado
### by Corina A. Santistevan

The village of Llano Quemado sits on the brow of a hill which is the south side of a valley through which runs what was first called "el Rio de las Trampas," now known as the little Rio Grande or the Ranchos River. It is a short distance from the confluence of the Rio Chiquito which comes from the east past Talpa.

Names of places have changed through the years and this has caused some confusion. According to oral history, the name of the village, Llano Quemado (burnt plain), was given to the Taos County settlement because some of the first settlers on this ridge came from Llano Quemado, earlier called El Pueblo Quemado, now named Cordova, in Rio Arriba County.

The valley of Llano Quemado, now Cordova, is not large. It is easy to understand that as more and more settlers came to the valley and as families grew, the need for land would drive some of them to seek it elsewhere. They often traded with the Taos settlers and Taos Indians. As they crossed Picuris Mountain on their way to Taos they came through Miranda Cañon and exited to the Llano Quemado ridge  They could see the lush green valley below them as they followed the ridge and the Ranchos River west to its junction with the Pueblo River at Los Cordovas.

Lorin Brown, a Taos historian, wrote that the first settlers tilled and tended their fields in the summer on the Taos Valley side of the mountain and left to spend the winter at Llano Quemado in Rio Arriba, at Peñasco and probably at other villages south of Taos. When they decided to establish a village of their own in the Taos Valley, the first settlers built their homes on a ridge overlooking the valley just as their ancestors had done in the  first Llano Quemado in Rio Arriba County. Brown lived in both Cordova and Taos and he recorded facts and folklore of both villages for the WPA Writers' Project.[5]

Folklore and a few statements found here and there in historical literature indicate that there may have been more than one chapel built to honor Our Lady of Mount Carmel in Llano Quemado. Don Abenicio Romero, long-time resident of Llano, showed the author and Helen Green Blumenschein the ruins near his home which he said was an early chapel of Llano Quemado. Other residents of Llano say they were told by grandparents that there had been another chapel but they do not know where it was located.

In the early 1700's the Comanche tribe began to drive the Apaches further and further south. Some of them sought shelter near Spanish settlements. In 1726, Captain Pedro de Rivera, who had been sent to New Mexico to deal with the Indian problem, wrote a letter to the viceroy in which he recommended moving the Jicarilla Apaches near Taos, so that their strength, together with that of the Spanish and the Taos Pueblo inhabitants, might serve as a barrier to the Comanches.[6]  His advice was not followed then but H. H. Bancroft in his *History of Arizona and New Mexico* writes that "...a mission of Jicarilla Apaches was founded on the Rio Trampas, three or four leagues from Taos in 1733, prospering for a time under Padre Marabal."[7] This could have been the first chapel of Llano Quemado as the Rio Trampas, now Ranchos River, runs from east to west below the ridge of Llano Quemado.

However, Fray Juan Agustin de Morfi in his *Geographical Description of New Mexico* states that Father Custodian Fray Josef de Velasco founded a mission five leagues to the north of Taos in 1733. It is not likely that there would have been two missions built to shelter the Jicarillas that close to each other in the very same year.[8]

It has not been possible to find any further reference to a mission built for the Jicarilla Apaches at either of the sites mentioned above. However, the report of the canonical visitor from Durango is worth noting. When Bishop Pedro Tamarón y Romeral made his episcopal visit to New Mexico in 1760, he described his entrance into Taos Pueblo in these words:

"The titular patron of this Indian pueblo is San Jerónimo. To reach it we traveled through pine forests and mountains until we descended to the spacious and beautiful valley they call the valley of Taos. In this valley we kept finding encampments of peaceful infidel Apache Indians who have sought the protection of the Spaniards so that they may defend them from the Comanches. Then we came to a river called Trampas which carries enough water."[9]

Bishop Tamaron did not mention a chapel, church or mission built for the Apaches living in those encampments. Neither did Fray Francisco Atanacio Domínguez when he visited all of the missions in his custody in New Mexico and made a thorough report on the economics of the area as well as the spiritual state of the missions. In 1776 he visited San Gerónimo de Taos and made a complete inventory of the mission and a census of the Taos Valley. He did not mention a mission for the Jicarilla Apaches near el Rio de Las Trampas.[10]

It seems probable that there really may have been a capilla built for Jicarilla Apaches as Bancroft stated but that it may have been small and perhaps not even in use by the time Bishop Domínguez visited the valley. If so, that may be the one that Don Abenicio Romero and others remember. The Apaches did not stay in any one place for very long. Some of them went to Pecos, some to El Cuartelejo and some joined other tribes.

Many changes were taking place for the settlers during the late 1700's and the early 1800's. By 1779 the fortified plaza of Ranchos de Taos was being finished. In 1786 Governor Juan Bautista de Anza was successful in defeating the Comanches and making a peace treaty with them and the threat to both Pueblo Indians and the settlers began to diminish.[11] The life of the settlers at Llano Quemado and in the whole valley of Taos became more peaceful but never safe from surprise attacks by small bands of Indians who were either ignorant of the treaties or chose not to respect them.

Changes were taking place in the government also. In 1821 Mexico declared its independence from Spain and for the brief period of twenty five years New Mexico was under Mexican rule. The changes during this period were hardly noticeable. Spanish was still the legal and dominant language, the alcaldes continued to mete out justice locally while the commandant general and governor handled the political and military administration. The biggest change came in 1846 when New Mexico was occupied by the United States armed forces. Now the settlers had to adjust to a new language and a new form of government.

The church too was changing. The priests were no longer Franciscan friars. Instead they were secular priests, a few of whom were native sons. The hierarchy of the church changed when, in 1850, Pope Pius IX established the Vicarate Apostolic of New Mexico and named Father Jean Baptiste Lamy as Vicar Apostolic. When Lamy came to Santa Fe he brought some French priests with him and others followed.[12] Now the settlers of Llano Quemado had new policies to follow in both church and civic government and new languages to learn.

In the Taos valley many chapels were being built. The Ranchos church, which was to become the mother church, was licensed to be built in 1813 and was in use by 1815; Our Lady of St. John of the Lakes was built in 1828; the private chapel of Our Lady of Talpa in 1838. It seems strange that the Llano Quemado settlers would not have been building a chapel of their own at this time unless they were using "the chapel built for the Jicarillas" if there was one. True, they were not very far from the Ranchos church but a capilla then as now served the faithful in many different ways. It is a physical shelter as well as a spiritual center. People gather there in groups to pray rosaries or novenas or they come singly to light a candle or say a prayer. The need for a capilla grows as soon as there is a cluster of homes with people who have communal or individual spiritual needs.

The two church documents which we have are confusing rather than enlightening. In one ot them, dated 1856, Bishop Lamy requests that papers on all private chapels from Taos and other missions be sent to him. In Taos he specifically asked for the chapels of Ranchos de Taos, Rio Chiquito and the Carmen Oratory at Llano de Talpa.[13]

Father Damaso Taladrid, who had replaced Padre Antonio José Martinez in Taos, wrote a letter to Lamy dated July 24, 1856. He begins by saying he is remitting "seis pesos" for the last license issued to "el oratorio del Llano bajo el titulo de Nuestra Señora de Carmen" (to the Llano oratorio under the title of Our Lady of Carmen). This does not mean that this was necessarily for a new chapel as licenses were granted now and then for the continuation of services. The word "last" implies that there may have been others granted earlier. The other two requests Father Taladrid makes in the same letter do not help to identify which

*Illustration 8:2—Woodcut of apse of the chapel of Nuestra Señora del Carmen. By Helen Blumenschein.*

oratory he is talking about. He recommends a very fine carpenter and asks the bishop if he would send someone to accompany said carpenter to visit other parishes to get ideas so that he might design the altar, two colaterals (altar screens) and a confessional. He asks also for a pair of silver cruets, an incensor and a small silver plate just like the ones he had sent to Ranchos.[14] Was all of this for a new chapel in 1856, for the chapel Brown states was built in 1852 or was it for the old "Jicarilla mission chapel" that was being reconstructed?

We do know that on June 30, 1864, a citizen of Llano Quemado, Antonio Ramon Medina, deeded to "el Illustrisimo Don Juan Bautista Lamy" a tract of land in Llano Quemado for a chapel to be built and dedicated to Our Lady of Mt. Carmel. In beautiful words he speaks of his devotion to the Virgin Mary and to his church. Then he proceeds to specify the borders of the site where the present capilla now stands.[15] The settlers of Llano Quemado did build this capilla although we do not know when the work was started or when it was finished.

The chapel of Our Lady of Mount Carmel is interesting both historically and architecturally. The chapel was built in the traditional rectangular shape but the sanctuary is apsidal, a semi-circular form which was not usually found in colonial New Mexico. It was used in only two other chapels in the state. The design may have been influenced by French priests.[16]

The interior of the chapel is now furnished with the white and gold trimmed European-style altar and screen. The original retable is now owned by the Society for the Preservation of Spanish Colonial Arts now on loan to the Museum of New Mexico and displayed in the Palace of the Governors Museum in Santa Fe. It was sold to the Society in 1928 when money was sorely needed to repair the roof.

*8:5—Parishoners plastering the walls of the chapel of Nuestra Señora del Carmen. No date. Archives of the church of St. Francis of Assisi.*

*8:6—Front of chapel of Nuestra Señora del Carmen. Photograph by the author. July 28, 1994.*

E. Boyd has identified the santero as Rafael Aragón whose reversed initials appear on the lunette of the Holy Ghost. The style is similar to other work he did in Santa Cruz, Cordova, San Miguel del Vado, Chama and other places.[17]

A report on the condition of the reredos shortly after it was purchased stated that the altar on which it rested was made of rough boards, badly rotted and not worth saving. It said that a new altar which made use of stock moldings had been constructed by a village carpenter. At the time of the report the santero was mistakenly identified as Miguel Aragón.[18]

The feast of Our Lady of Mount Carmel is celebrated each year on the fifteenth and sixteenth of July. Vespers are said on the evening of the fifteenth followed by a procession of the faithful carrying Our Lady of Mount Carmel and other visiting santos from the neighboring chapels and St. Francis, the mother church. The parishoners walk south towards the mountains on a road lined with farolitos and luminarias. The following day mass is celebrated and scapulars are given to the congregation as a symbol of Our Lady of Mount Carmel. The procession with Our Lady then goes down to a communal feast at St. Francis Gymnasium. In the past every home prepared a feast and relatives and visitors went to honor many different homes during the day. The chapel continues to be a source of pride for the villagers.

8:7—*Rear of chapel in Llano Quemado showing the round apse reminiscent of French churches. Photograph by John Martin Campbell. July 28, 1994.*

8:8—*Retable sold to the Spanish Colonial Arts Society in 1928 that is now on display in the Palace of the Governors in Santa Fe. Courtesy of the Museum of New Mexico. 1528.*

*8:9—The present sanctuary. Photograph by John Martin Campbell. July 28, 1994.*

The Chapel of San Isidro, Patron Saint of Farmers
at Los Cordovas/Cordillera
by Corina A. Santistevan

The Chapel of San Isidro, patron saint of farmers, was built in 1951–52, on land donated by Benjamin and Josefina Sanchez. They were heirs of Don Pedro Sanchez, a well-known philanthropist and biographer of the life of Padre José Antonio Martinez.

The chapel is on the Quijosa grant. This grant has been known by various names, as was the owner of the grant, Francisca Guijosa, Gijosa, Equijosa or Aquijosa. Under Spanish law and administration women did have protected property rights. Some women were very successful at buying, trading and owning large tracts of land and stock. In 1715 Francisca petitioned Governor Juan Ignacio Flores Mogollon for a grant to a tract of land in the Taos valley. In October of that year she was placed in possession of it by the lieutenant governor. It extended from the Rio Pueblo in the north to Picuris on the south, to the black rocks of an arroyo hondo on the west to the middle road on the east. In 1725 she sold it to one of the early settlers of Los Cordovas, Baltazar Trujillo.[20]

Los Cordovas, itself, is of historic importance. The Spanish chroniclers speak of coming onto this vast plain after crossing the mountains and following the course of the rivers. Whether they came out of Miranda Canyon or out of Rio Chiquito, they could follow the Rio Grande del Rancho to where it joins the Rio de Pueblo in Los Cordovas and they could follow that to the Pueblo of San Geronimo de Taos.

Some of the same friends and families of the Llano Quemado now Cordova, in Rio Arriba County, who settled in Llano Quemado, Taos County, went furthur west and settled Los Cordovas. Many of the settlers were named Cordova and some of their descendants still live there. The conjunction of the five rivers that sweep through the valley creates a larger river that empties into the Rio Grande. This big river runs along the west side of the land in Los Cordovas making it possible for the settlers to farm on the east side and graze their livestock on the west bank.

A large residence was built on a commanding site on top of a low hill for Don Juan Felipe Romero, an important member of the Spanish colonial village. It was planned as a ten-room quadrangle with a central patio. The back courtyard was enclosed by rock walls, some of which can still be seen. A torreon was built on the west side of the compound for protection. Two rooms on the southeast side of the compound were later used as a private chapel. The patron saint was San Isidro. Although it was a private chapel, it was used by the communities of Los Cordovas and Cordillera for many years. The part of the building where the chapel was located still stands. It is no longer used as a chapel but as a residence. The altars were removed and fireplaces built in their place. The chapel, or oratorio, is listed in the New Mexico Register of Cultural Properties and the National Register of Historic Places.[19]

The chapel that now serves the communities of Los Cordovas and Cordillera is a simple adobe structure with a flat roof and a double door facing west. It is a rectangle with three windows on each side of the nave. The windows face northwest and southeast. On the north side there is a small sacristy.

The woodwork inside was done by some of the craftsmen of the village. The retable in the sanctuary, made of native wood, was made by Emilio Martinez in the early 1950's. Since then an altar of pine and cedar has been added as well as two side nichos for the statues of Mary and Joseph.

*Illustration 8:3—A woodcut of the old Oratorio of San Isidro by Helen Blumenschein.*

*8:10—Exterior of chapel of San Isidro.
Photograph by James Griffin.*

On either side of the center panel with its wooden nicho as the tabernacle are two new retables made by Roger Trujillo, a young man who is following the tradition of the old santeros. One of them depicts St. Francis in front of the Ranchos church; the other has San Isidro in front of the Los Cordovas/Cordillera chapel. On the back walls are two cedar plaques on which are placed the names of all the parishioners who have served as stewards (mayordomos) of the chapel and all the names of benefactors.

The feast day of San Isidro is celebrated on the fifteenth of May. The blessing of the fields takes place after vespers on the day before the feast day. A procession with the patron saint and the patron saints of Talpa, Llano Quemado and Ranchos moves from the chapel either east or west on a road lined with farolitos and luminarias. The next day the procession goes in the opposite direction. Upon its return to the chapel, the entriega is sung. This is a hymn sung especially for this occasion which gives thanks to the past year's mayordomos, welcomes the new ones and encourages everyone to honor the patron saint. The past year mayordomos present San Isidro in his carryall to the new mayordomos, while the entriega is being sung.

## *GLOSSARY*

**adobe**. Unburnt sun-dried brick.

**alis**. Plaster finish applied with sheepskin.

**apse**. Semi-circular or polygonal projection of a church
housing the altar.

**araña**. A kind of chandelier to hold candles made with two cross
pieces of wood.

**ayuda de parroquia**. Chapel or mission.

**built-up-roof**. A continuous roof covering made up of plies of coated roofing
felts alternated with layers of pitch or asphalt and surfaced with gravel.

**bulto**. A carved wooden statue of a holy figure.

**buttress**. A structure, in this case made of adobe bricks, placed
against a wall to reinforce or support.

**caliche**. A hard soil layer containing calcium carbonate, found in deserts and
arid and semi-arid regions.

**camposanto**. Holy field. A cemetery.

**canale**. Spanish: **canal**. A word used by architects and historians in New
Mexico to identify a roof gutter or scupper extending through the parapet,
made from boards or hollowed logs, usually lined with sheet metal.

**canonical visitor**. A visitor sent by a bishop to inspect the diocese.

**capilla**. Chapel.

**clerestory window**. Window at the end of the nave, in the wall above the
roof at the crossing opposite the altar.

**colateral**. Retable. Word commonly used in church documents.

**corbel**. In New Mexican buildings, a shaped piece of timber placed under the
viga at the bearing wall extending out a few feet to strengthen the viga.
Sometimes carved.

**cordillera**. A chain of mountains.

**dado**. Lower portion of a wall decorated differently from the upper part, in
this case painted a darker color. Wainscot.

**diocese**. The district or churches under the jurisdiction of a bishop; a bishopric.

**embrasure**. An opening in a parapet for a gun.

**enjarradora**. Woman who plasters with mud.

**entrada**. Entrance.

**entriega**. (de Santo) Delivery of the patron saint to the mayordomos for the new
year. A special song sung for a certain occasion.

**farolito**. Diminutive of **farol** (lantern). A kind of festive light, a small fire in front of a building, a candle in a paper bag partially filled with sand. Often used interchangeably with luminaria.

**Fray**. A friar. A title used before names of men in religious orders.

**hacienda**. Farm, ranch, usually self-sustaining.

**husbandman**. Farmer.

**iglesia**. Church.

**latilla**. Small aspen or cottonwood limb, usually stripped of bark, placed over vigas to form a ceiling. Also savino.

**league**. A measure of distance equal to about three miles.

**lienzo**. Linen cloth.

**lintel**. A horizontal beam bridging an opening.

**Llano Quemado**. Burnt plain.

**luminaria**. Any of several festive lights which are displayed on special occasions such as Christmas or fiestas.

**mission**. A church and its attendant buildings used as a missionary station. Now commonly used for the outlying chapels of a parish.

**morada**. A Penitente chapel and chapter house.

**muntin**. A secondary framing member to hold panes within a window or glazed door.

**nave**. Central part of a church with a center aisle and usually side aisles, but not in most New Mexico mission churches. The space for the laity.

**nicho**. A small recess in a wall or altar screen usually used to house a bulto.

**oratorio**. A place for prayer, usually a small private chapel.

**parish**. An administrative part of a diocese that has its own church.

**parroquia**. Parish, parochial church.

**Penitente**. Regional name for a member of the Brotherhood of Light, a religious confraternity the origin of which is disputed by historians.

**pintle**. An upright pin or bolt used as a pivot, as for a door.

**plaza**. A square, a town, a fortified place enclosed by walls and/or buildings.

**pueblo**. Town, village, settlement.

**puerton**. A large gate.

**raja**. Split wood like a shingle used over vigas to form a ceiling and roof deck. Usually cedar.

**reredos**. Altar screen.

**retable**. Spanish: **retablo**. Altar screen.

**rubbing**. A representation of a raised or indented surface made by placing paper over the surface and rubbing the paper with a soft pencil, chalk or charcoal.

**sacristy**. A room in a church housing sacred vessels and vestments.

**sanctuary**. Most sacred part of a church, the space around the main altar.

**santero**. A person who paints or carves sacred figures.

**scapula**. Picture of a saint hung around the neck with a chain during certain ceremonies.

**stucco**. An exterior finish composed of portland cement, lime, and sand, which are mixed with water.

**terra alba**. White gypsum used in plaster and ceramics.

**tierra amarilla**. Yellow earth used for plaster.

**tierra blanca**. White earth, gypsum.

**tierra bayita**. Light, or sand colored earth. Usually the finish over adobe plaster applied with sheepskin.

**torreón**. A round fortified tower.

**transcept**. The transverse arms of a cross-shaped church between the nave and the apse.

**transom**. A horizontal bar across the opening of a window or door.

**viga**. A log of pine or fir used as a beam, usually stripped of bark, sometimes carved.

**visita**. A visitation, an ecclesiastical inspection.

## *References*

Cobos, Rubén, *A Dictionary of New Mexico and Southern Colorado Spanish,* Museum of New Mexico Press, Santa Fe, 1983.

Harris, Cyril M., *Dictionary of Architecture and Construction,* McGraw-Hill, Inc., 1975.

*Nuevo Pequeño Larousse Ilustrado Libreria Larousse,* Paris, France, 1960.

Weigle, Marta, and White, Peter, *The Lore of New Mexico,* University of New Mexico Press, Albuquerque, 1988.

Williams, Edwin B., *The New College Spanish and English Dictionary,* Amsco School Publications, Inc., New York, 1968.

# BIBLIOGRAPHY

## Abbreviations:

AASF—Archives of the Archdiocese of Santa Fe
LOC—Library of Congress
JGMA—John Gaw Meem Archive of Southwestern Architecture,
    University of New Mexico General Library
HABS—Historic American Buildings Survey
GWA—George Wright Associates (office files)

## CHAPTER 1

1. Pearce, T. M., *New Mexico Place Names*, University of New Mexico Press, Albuquerque, 1965, 162–163.
2. Millicent Rogers Museum, text from exhibit in preparation, Taos, 1991.
3. Wroth, William, *The Chapel of Our Lady of Talpa*, The Taylor Museum, Colorado Springs, 1979, 19, note 4.
4. Woosley, Anne I., "Puebloan Prehistory of the Northern Rio Grande Settlement Population, Subsistence." Quarterly Journal of the Arizona Archaeological and Historical Society, Vol. 51 No. 3, Spring, 1986, Tucson.
5. Boyer, Jeffrey L., "A Revised National Register Nomination for the Taos Pueblo National Historic Landmark," Taos, January 3, 1984.
6. Wroth, 16.
7. Jenkins, Myra Ellen, "Taos Pueblo and Its Neighbors," *New Mexico Historical Review*, 41: 85–114.
8. Wroth, 16.
9. Thomas, Alfred B., *After Coronado, Spanish Exploration Northeast of New Mexico, 1696–1727*, University of Oklahoma Press, Norman, 1935, 38–39.
10. Jenkins, 91.
11. Wroth, 16.
12. Adams, Eleanor B., "Bishop Tamarón's Visitation of New Mexico, 1760," Historical Society of New Mexico, Vol. XV, 1954.
13. Simmons, Marc, *New Mexico: A Bicentennial History*, Norton and Co. New York, 1977, 85–86.
14. Adams, 57–58.
15. Adams, Eleanor B. and Chavez, Fray Angelico, *The Missions of New Mexico, 1776, A Description By Fray Francisco Atanasio Domínguez with Other Contemporary Documents*, University of New Mexico Press, Albuquerque, 1956, reprinted 1975, 252.
16. Simmons, 86.
17. Adams, Chavez, 112–113.
18. D'Emilio, Sandra; Campbell, Susan; Kessell, John L, *Spirit and Vision, Images of Ranchos de Taos Church*, Museum of New Mexico Press, Santa Fe, 1987, 116.
19. D'Emilio, et al., 116.
20. Bunting, Bainbridge, *Early Architecture in New Mexico*, University of New Mexico Press, Albuquerque, 1978, 71.
21. Wroth, 18.
22. Wroth, 22.
23. Field, Matt, *Matt Field on the Santa Fe Trail*, Sunder, John E., editor, University of Oklahoma Press, Norman, 1960, 190–193.
24. Gonzales, Rachel, "Los Comanches and New Year's Day," Christmas in Taos, 1989.

25. Byrne, Most Rev. Edwin V., *Lamy Memorial*, Archdiocese of Santa Fe, Santa Fe, 1950.
26. Simmons, 119–131.
27. Wroth, 35.
28. Boyer, ibid.
29. Byrne, ibid.
30. Baxter, John O., National Register of Historic Places Inventory—Nomination Form, "Village of Ranchos de Taos," Santa Fe, June 25, 1976.
31. Sherman, John, *Taos, A Pictorial History*, William Gannon, Santa Fe, n.d., 35.
32. Martinez, Eva Rivera, and Santistevan, Corina, interview, Ranchos de Taos, August 16, 1990.
33. Boyer, ibid.
34. Santistevan, Corina, "Reverend Jose A. Garcia First Pastor at San Francisco de Asis Church at Ranchos de Taos, N. M.," not published.
35. Santistevan, Corina, conversation, Ranchos de Taos, 1990.
36. Correspondence between Archbishop R. A. Gerken and Fr. José A. Garcia, June 1, 1937 through August 20, 1937. AASF.
37. Garcia to Gerken, letter, April 17, 1939. AASF.
38. The Taos Artists' Association to Archbishop Gerken, telegram, Taos, July 6, 1939. AASF.
39. *The New Mexican*, Santa Fe, July 10, 1939.
40. Miles, John, to Archbishop Gerken, letter, Santa Fe, July 10, 1939. AASF.
41. Martinez and Santisteven, ibid.
42. Benrimo, Dorothy, and Haegler, Tonnie, documented conversation, Ranchos de Taos, early 1960's. AASF.
43. Harbert, Ben F., to Gerken, letter, Taos, July 14, 1939. AASF.
44. *The New Mexican*, Santa Fe, July 15, 1939.
45. *The New Mexican*, Santa Fe, July 18, 1939.
46. *El Taoseño*, Taos, November 15, 1939.
47. Wright, George S., Architect, 1967, GWA.

## CHAPTER 2

1. D'Emilio, et al., 117–118.
2. Kubler, George, *The Religious Architecture of New Mexico*, Taylor Museum of the Colorado Springs Fine Arts Center, Colorado Springs, 1940. Reprint, University of New Mexico Press, Albuquerque, 1972, 103–104.
3. Prince, L. Bradford, *Spanish Mission Churches of New Mexico*, Rio Grande Press, Glorieta, N. M., Reprint, 1977, 261.
4. "The Old Mission: St. Francis of Assisi," pamphlet, Amarillo, Texas, n.d.
5. D'Emilio, et al., 119.
6. Santistevan, Corina, "Fray Jose Benito Pereyro," unpublished.
7. D'Emilio, et al., 117–120.
8. Kubler, 60.
9. Boyd, E., *Popular Arts of New Mexico*, Museum of New Mexico Press, Santa Fe, 1974. 357.
10. Kubler, 35–37, 66.
11. Historic American Buildings Survey (HABS) drawings, 36NM7, "Mission Church at Ranchos de Taos, New Mexico," U. S. Department of the Interior, Washington, D. C., 1934. Sheet 3, 11, 12. JGMA
12. Kubler, 66–70.
13. Abert, J. W., "Report of His Examination of New Mexico in the Years 1846–47," Senate Executive Document 23, 30th Congress, 1848.
14. Adams, Chavez, 113.

15. McHenry, Paul G., Jr., *Adobe and Rammed Earth Buildings*, John Wylie and Sons, University of Arizona Press, Tucson, 1984, 6.

16. Boyd, 2, 3.

17. Kubler, 25.

18. McHenry, 67.

19. Kubler, 83–84.

20. Kubler, 32–34.

21. Fitchen, John, *Building Construction Before Mechanization,* MIT Press, Cambridge, 1986, 84–95.

22. Ivey, James E., *In the Midst of a Loneliness: The Architectural History of the Salinas Missions*, National Park Service Southwest Cultural Resources Center, Papers #15, Santa Fe, 1988, 53–54.

23. Bunting, 8.

24. Fernandez, Gustavo, and Santistevan, Corina, taped interview, Ranchos de Taos, September 16, 1990.

25. Adams, Chavez, 13–14, 103.

26. Bunting, 72.

27. Adams, Chavez, 14.

28. HABS, Sheet 26.

29. Fernandez and Santistevan.

30. Bunting, 67.

31. Garcia, Rev. José, "Symphony in Mud," Special Coronado Issue,  Kit Carson Edition, *Taos Review*, July 18, 1940.

32. Santistevan, Corina, conversation, Ranchos de Taos.

33. Ewing, Dr. Rodney, report to Van Dorn Hooker, October 24, 1990.

34. Fernandez and Santistevan.

35. HABS, Sheet 11.

36. Adams, Chavez, 104.

37. Santistevan, conversation.

38. Boyd, 48.

39. D'Emilio, et al., 123.

40. Gerken, Anthony to Fr. José Garcia, letter, Ranchos de Taos, April 25, 1938.  AASF.

41. Garcia, José, to Archbishop R. A. Gerken, letter, Ranchos de  Taos, December 18, 1938.  AASF

42. HABS, Sheet 1.

43. Fernandez and Santistevan.

44. Luhan, Mabel Dodge, *Edge of Taos Desert*, Harcourt Brace and  Co., 1937, University of New Mexico Press reprint, Albuquerque, 1987, 83, 88–91.

45. D'Emilio, et al., 121.

46. Ibid., 122–123.

47. Boyd, 356.

48. D'Emilio, et al., 122.

## CHAPTER 3

1. Garcia, "Symphony."

2. Sherman, 30.

3. Howlett, W. J., *Life of Bishop Macheboeuf*, Pueblo, Colorado, 1908, Franklin Press reprint edited by Thomas J. Steele, S. J., and Ronald S. Brockway, 1987, 171, 205.

4. HABS, Sheets 26, 27, 28.

5. HABS, Sheets 19 to 26.

6. Kubler, 45–46.

7. Ibid., 45.

8. HABS, Sheets 14, 20.

9. Kubler, Photograph 136.

10. Garcia, "Symphony."

11. HABS, Sheet 6, notes.

12. Ibid., Sheet 18.

13. Rudisill, Richard, *Photographers of the New Mexico Territory 1854–1912*, Museum of New Mexico, Santa Fe, 1973, 22.

14. Luhan, 85.

15. HABS, Sheets 6, 7, 12, notes.

16. D'Emilio, et al., 37, Plate 6.

17. Luhan, 84.

18. HABS, Sheet 6, notes.

19. Garcia, Rev. José, to Archbishop Rudolph A. Gerken, letter, Ranchos de Taos, July 1, 1938. AASF

20. Meem, John Gaw, to Gerken, letter, Santa Fe, July 14, 1938. AASF

21. Garcia to Gerken, letter, Ranchos de Taos, August 9, 1938. AASF

22. Meem to Garcia, letter, Santa Fe, August 15, 1938. AASF

23. Rev. Hatch, Paul V., to Archbishop Edwin V. Byrne, letter, Ranchos de Taos, September 15, 1949. AASF

24. Garcia, "Symphony."

25. Rev. Galli, Clarence F., to Msgr. Reinberg, Francis, letters, May 18 and May 31, 1960. AASF

26. Galli to Byrne, letter, April 4, 1961. AASF

27. Galli and Reinberg, correspondence, May 9 to September 1, 1961. AASF

28. Fernandez, Santistevan.

29. Fernandes, Santistevan.

30. Reinberg to Rev. Alvarez, Manuel, letter, Albuquerque, October 25, 1965. AASF

31. Santistevan, conversation, ibid.

## CHAPTER 4

1. Conron, John, editor, "Conservation: Ranchos de Taos Church," *New Mexico Architecture*, Vol. 5, Nos. 9 and 10, Sept.–Oct., 1963.

2. Hooker, Van Dorn, "To Hand Plaster or Not??," *New Mexico Architecture*, Vol. 19, No. 5, Sept.–Oct., 1977.

3. Wright, George S., Taos Notes, Sept. 9, 1966. GWA

4. Wright, George S., "Report on Existing Conditions and Recommendations for Remedial Action—Ranchos de Taos Church," Albuquerque, Oct. 21, 1966. GWA

5. Hooker, "To Hand Plaster."

6. Stout, M. Kent, "Inspection Report," Jan. 29, 1967. GWA

7. Bottorff, Leslie, "Church Restoration Stirs Passions," *Taos News*, Feb. 2, 1967.

8. Janssen, Genevieve, to Archbishop James Peter Davis, letter, Taos, Feb. 3, 1967. GWA

9. Heaton, Mrs. Sammy, to Davis, letter, Ranchos de Taos, Feb. 6, 1967. GWA

10. "Archbishop's Permission Needed for Church Soft-Plastering Fund," *Taos News,* Feb. 9, 1967.

11. Wright, to Janssen, letter, Albuquerque, Feb. 13, 1967. GWA

12. Fernandez, Gustavo, to Davis, letter, Ranchos de Taos, Feb. 15, 1967. GWA

13. Wright, report.

14. Sigler, Charles, to Stout, letter, San Francisco, Feb. 16, 1967. GWA

15. Johnson, Orval B., to Stout, letter, Sacramento, Feb. 27, 1967. GWA

16. Meem, John Gaw, to Janssen, letter, Santa Fe, Feb. 8, 1967. GWA

17. "Stucco on Taos Church? It's Sacrilegious!", *Albuquerque Tribune*, Feb. 23, 1967.

18. "Ranchos 'Misunderstanding'...Hard Plaster Last Resort," *Taos News*, Feb. 23, 1967.

19. Meem, to Wright, letter, Santa Fe, Mar. 13, 1967. GWA

20  Meem, to Janssen, letter, Santa Fe, Apr. 14, 1967. GWA

21. Burch, Vee, "Hard Plastering Marks End of Era in Traditional Adobe Architecture," *El Paso Times*, "Sundial," Aug. 13, 1967.

22. Wright, to Hooker, letter, Arlington, Texas, Aug. 1, 1974.

23. Wirth, Nancy Meem, conversation with Hooker, Santa Fe, 1990.


## CHAPTER 5

1. Hooker, Van Dorn, "Restoration Work at Saint Francis of Assisi Church, Ranchos de Taos," *New Mexico Architecture*, Vol. 8 No. 3, May–June, 1987.

2. Nestor, Robert, to Father Michael O'Brien, letter, Santa Fe, March 22, 1978.

3. Nestor, notes of telephone conversation with O'Brien, February 6, 1979.

4. Johnson Nestor Architects, Spears, Beverly, "A Report on the Exterior Plaster," Santa Fe, March 17, 1979.

5. Nestor, Field Report, Ranchos de Taos, June 27, 1979.

6. Gonzales, L. J. V., to Archbishop Robert Sanchez, letter, Ranchos de Taos, July 3, 1979. AASF

7. O'Brien to Sanchez, letter, Ranchos de Taos, July 9, 1979. AASF

8. Sanchez to Gonzales, letter, Albuquerque, July 10, 1979. AASF

9. Johnson Nestor, notes of conversation with O'Brien, August 17, 1979.

10. Hooker, O'Brien, conversations, 1979 to 1990.

11. Ibid.

12. Pogzeba, Wolfgang, *Ranchos de Taos: San Francisco de Asis Church*, Lowell Press, Kansas City, MO, 1981, 38.

13. Hooker, O'Brien, conversations.

14. Pogzeba, 42.

15. Daigh, Janice, "Thanks Will be Given at Mass," *Taos News*, October 4, 1979.

16. Ibid.

17. "A Church May Crumble, But Spirit is Strong," *Sangre de Cristo Chronicle*, October 11, 1979.


## CHAPTER 6

1. Boyd, *Popular Arts,* 352–356.

2. Boyd, E. "Museum Conservation Project at Ranchos de Taos," *El Palacio*, Vol. 60, No. 12, December, 1953.

3. Boyd, *Popular Arts*, 157, 349-353, 356.

4. Prince, 261.

5. WPA Writers Program, *New Mexico—A Guide to the Colorful State*, American Guide Series, Hastings House, New York, 1940.

6. Boyd, "Museum Conservation."

7. Boyd, *Popular Arts*, 353.

8. Boyd, "Museum Conservation."

9. Hooker, conversations with O'Brien.

10. Daigh, Janice, "Altar Screen Restored for St. Francis Celebration," *Taos News*, Oct. 8, 1981.

11. Hooker, O'Brien.


## CHAPTER 7

1. Wroth, 24–26.

2. Wroth, 81–84.

3. Harney, Andy Leon, "Racing Against Oblivion," *Historic Preservation*, Jan.–Feb., 1983.

4. Peterson, Charles E., "Relief Employment, etc.," memorandum.Washington, Nov. 13, 1933. JGMA

5. The Historic American Buildings Survey, pamphlet, U. S. Department of the Interior and the National Park Service, Washington, 1936. JGMA
6. Meem, John Gaw, to Peterson, letter, Santa Fe, Nov. 25, 1933. JGMA
7. Williamson, George H., to Meem, letter, Denver, Dec. 11, 1933. JGMA
8. Meem to Williamson, letter, Santa Fe, Dec. 13, 1933. JGMA
9. Meem to Vint, Thomas C., telegram, Santa Fe, Dec. 27, 1933. JGMA
10. Vint to Meem, letter, Washington, Dec. 28, 1933. JGMA
11. HABS Circular No. 1, Washington, Dec. 12, 1933. JGMA
12. Meem to Hyde, Leicester, letter, Santa Fe, Dec. 26, 1933. JGMA
13. District Order No. 36, "List of Projects for New Mexico," unsigned, to Vint, Santa Fe, Jan. 5, 1934. JGMA
14. Hyde to Vint, letter, Santa Fe, Jan. 3, 1934. JGMA
15. Hornbein, Victor, notes, Denver, 1983.
16. HABS, Sheet 1.
17. Historic American Buildings Survey, drawings, La Capilla de Nuestra Señora de Talpa, Talpa, New Mexico, 36NM10, U. S. Department of the Interior, Washington, D. C., 1934. JGMA
18. Hornbein.
19. HABS, St. Francis, Sheets 1-32.
20. Hornbein.
21. Fisher, Alan, "New Mexico Interlude, The Documentation of a Death Mask," notes for a talk in Denver, n. d. JGMA

## CHAPTER 8

1. Miller, Michael, *Monuments of Adobe*, Taylor Publishing Co., Dallas, Texas, 1991, 51.
2. Wroth, 24–26.
3. Boyd, *Popular Arts,* 361.
4. Boyd, *Popular Arts,* 357, 360–361.
5. Brown, Lorin, with C. L. Briggs and M. Weigle, "Alto Huachin," *Hispanic Folklife of New Mexico*, University of New Mexico Press, Albuquerque, 1978. 55
6. Thomas, Alfred B., *Forgotten Frontiers*, University of Oklahoma Press, Norman, 1932, 58.
7. Bancroft, Hubert H., *History of Arizona and New Mexico, 1530–1888*, The History Company, San Francisco, 1889.
8. Thomas, 242.
9. Adams, 56.
10. Adams, Chavez, 112.
11. D'Emilio et al., 116.
12. Byrne, Most Rev. Edwin V., *Lamy Memorial*, Archdiocese of Santa Fe, Santa Fe, 1950.
13. AASF, LD 1856.
14. AASF, roll 56, frames 524–526.
15. Taos County Records, Book 26A.
16. Kubler, 148.
17. Boyd, *Popular Arts,* 402. Also *El Palacio*, Jan. 4–25, nos. 1–4.
18. Applegate, Frank G., "Altarpiece from Llano Quemado," Report to Society for Protection of Spanish Colonial Art, n.d.
19. Weigle, Marta, ed. *Hispanic Arts and Ethnohistory in the Southwest*, Ancient City Press, Santa Fe, 1983, 336–337.
20. Muller, Anna, National Register of Historic Places—Nomination Form, "San Ysidro Oratorio or Los Cordovas Chapel," August, 1982.

*DRAWINGS PREPARED BY*
*THE HISTORIC AMERICAN BUILDINGS SURVEY*
*1934*

Mission Church at Ranchos de Taos, New Mexico
St. Francis of Assisi Church, 32 sheets.
Pages 117–148


La Capilla de Nuestra Senora de Talpa, Talpa, New Mexico
The Chapel of Our Lady of Talpa, 12 sheets.
Pages 149–160.

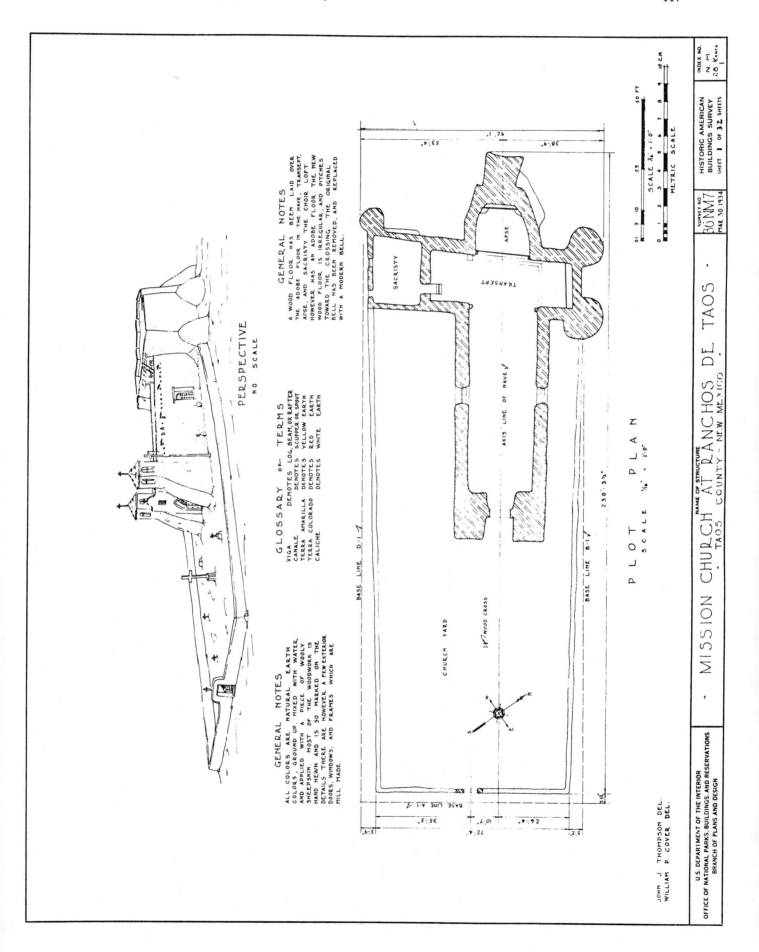

PERSPECTIVE

NO SCALE

GENERAL NOTES

A WOOD FLOOR HAS BEEN LAID OVER THE ADOBE FLOOR IN THE NAVE, TRANSEPT, APSE, AND SACRISTY. THE CHOIR LOFT HOWEVER HAS AN ADOBE FLOOR. THE NEW WOOD FLOOR IS IRREGULAR, AND PITCHES TOWARD THE CROSSING. THE ORIGINAL BELL HAS BEEN REMOVED, AND REPLACED WITH A MODERN BELL.

GLOSSARY of TERMS

VIGA          DENOTES LOG, BEAM, OR RAFTER
CANALE        DENOTES SCUPPER OR SPOUT
TERRA AMARILLA  DENOTES YELLOW EARTH
TERRA COLORADO  DENOTES RED EARTH
CALICHE       DENOTES WHITE EARTH

GENERAL NOTES

ALL COLORS ARE NATURAL EARTH COLORS, GROUND UP, MIXED WITH WATER, AND APPLIED WITH A PIECE OF WOOLY SHEEPSKIN. MOST OF THE WOODWORK IS HAND HEWN AND IS SO MARKED ON THE DETAILS. THERE ARE HOWEVER A FEW EXTERIOR DOORS, WINDOWS, AND FRAMES WHICH ARE MILL MADE.

PLOT PLAN

SCALE ⅛" = 1'-0"

CHURCH YARD

SACRISTY

APSE

TRANSEPT

AXIS LINE OF NAVE

BASE LINE D-1

BASE LINE B-1

BASE LINE A-1

WOOD CROSS

SCALE 3/32" = 1'-0"

METRIC SCALE

SURVEY NO
36 NM7
MAR 30, 1934

HISTORIC AMERICAN
BUILDINGS SURVEY
SHEET 1 OF 32 SHEETS

INDEX NO.
N.M.
26 Kawa
1

NAME OF STRUCTURE
· MISSION CHURCH AT RANCHOS DE TAOS ·
· TAOS COUNTY - NEW MEXICO ·

U.S. DEPARTMENT OF THE INTERIOR
OFFICE OF NATIONAL PARKS, BUILDINGS, AND RESERVATIONS
BRANCH OF PLANS AND DESIGN

JOHN J. THOMPSON DEL.
WILLIAM P. COVER DEL.

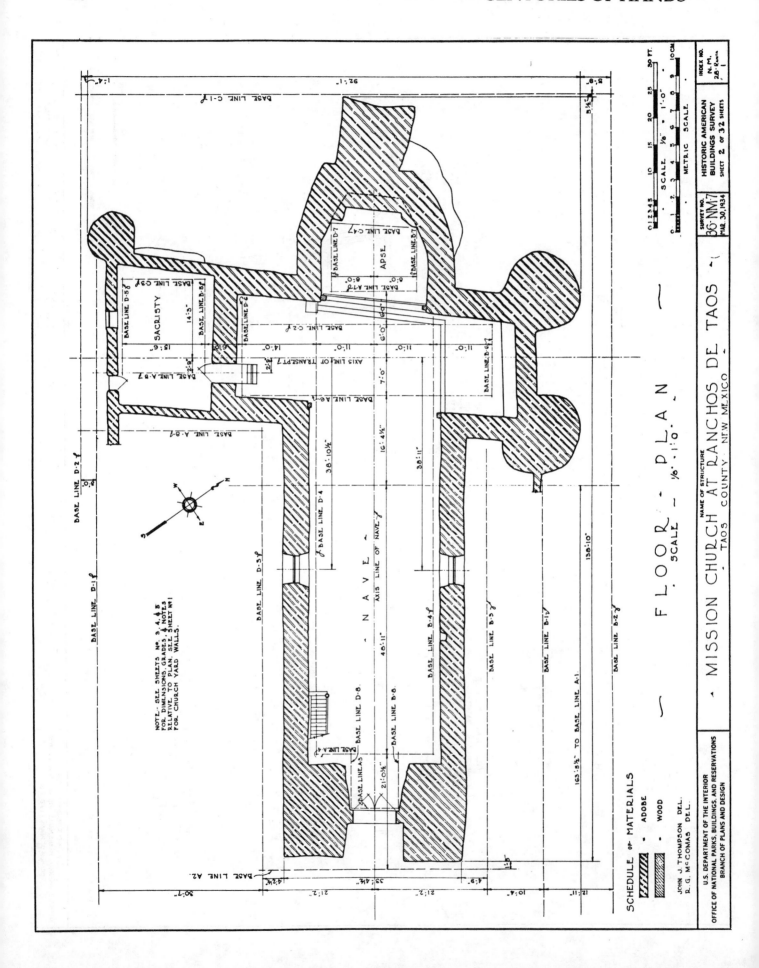

FLOOR · PLAN
SCALE ~ ⅛" = 1'-0"

MISSION CHURCH AT RANCHOS DE TAOS
~ TAOS COUNTY, NEW MEXICO ~

SCHEDULE OF MATERIALS

- ADOBE
- WOOD

JOHN J. THOMPSON  DEL.
R. G. McCOMAS  DEL.

U.S. DEPARTMENT OF THE INTERIOR
OFFICE OF NATIONAL PARKS, BUILDINGS, AND RESERVATIONS
BRANCH OF PLANS AND DESIGN

HISTORIC AMERICAN
BUILDINGS SURVEY
SHEET 2 OF 32 SHEETS

SURVEY NO.
36·NM·7
MAR. 30, 1934

INDEX NO.
N. M.
28·Ranta
1

NOTE – SEE SHEETS Nos. 3, 4, & 5
FOR DIMENSIONS, GRADES, & NOTES
RELATIVE TO PLAN. SEE SHEET No.1
FOR CHURCH YARD WALLS.

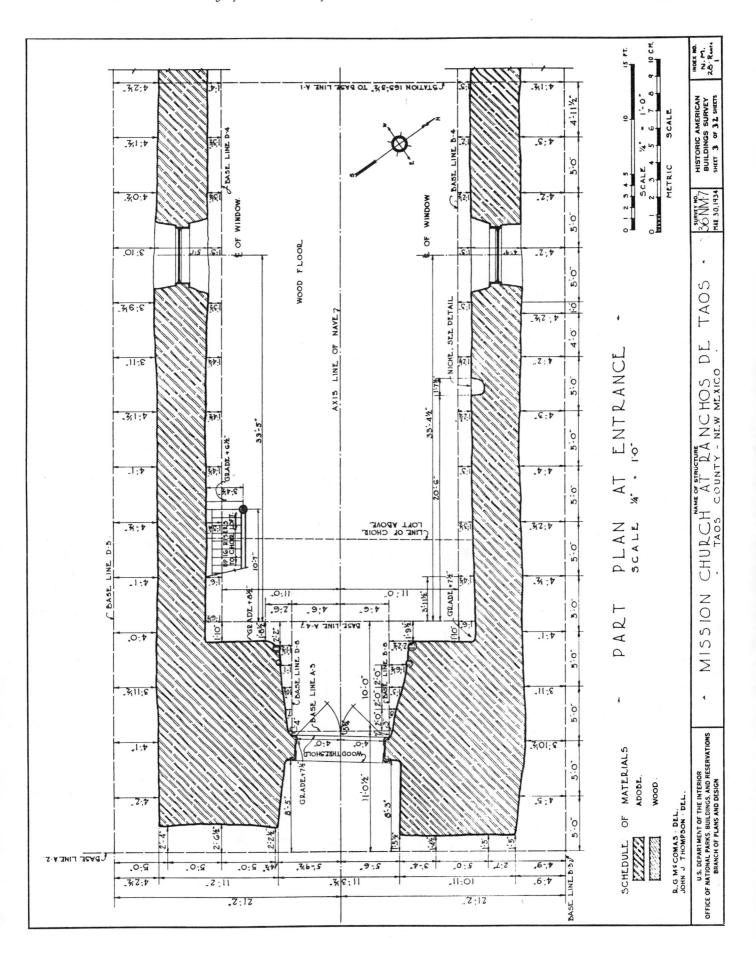

PART PLAN AT ENTRANCE
SCALE ¼" = 1'-0"

MISSION CHURCH AT RANCHOS DE TAOS
TAOS COUNTY - NEW MEXICO

SCHEDULE OF MATERIALS.
ADOBE.
WOOD.

R.G. McCOMAS · DEL.
JOHN J. THOMPSON · DEL.

U.S. DEPARTMENT OF THE INTERIOR
OFFICE OF NATIONAL PARKS, BUILDINGS, AND RESERVATIONS
BRANCH OF PLANS AND DESIGN

HISTORIC AMERICAN
BUILDINGS SURVEY
SHEET 3 OF 32 SHEETS

SURVEY NO. 36 NM 7
MAR. 30, 1934

INDEX NO.
N. M.
28-Rant.

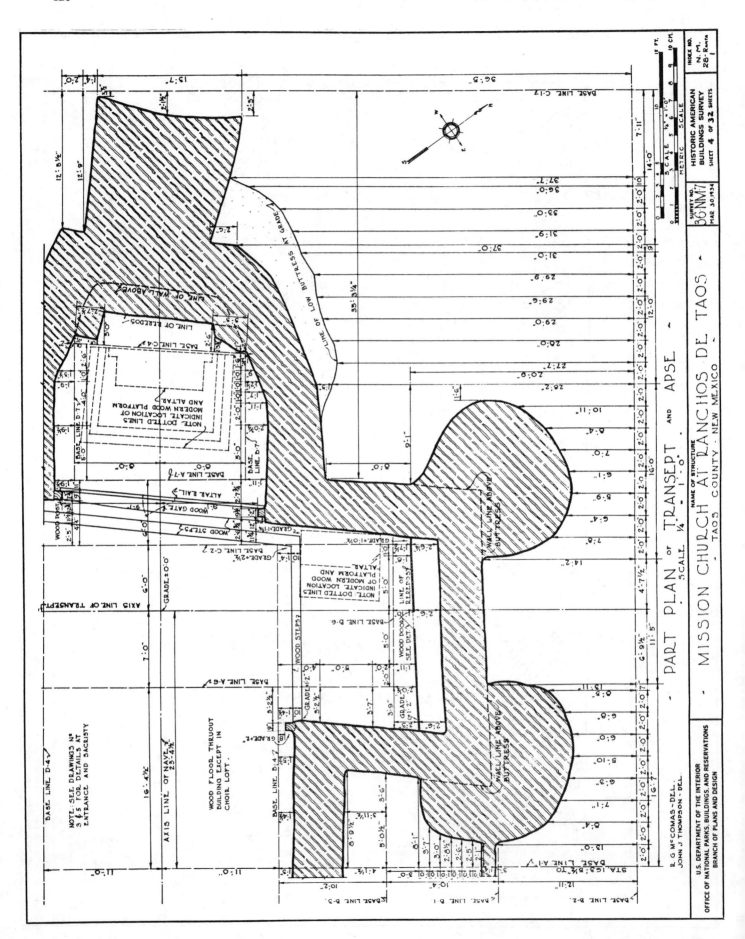

PART PLAN OF TRANSEPT AND APSE

MISSION CHURCH AT RANCHOS DE TAOS

TAOS COUNTY · NEW MEXICO

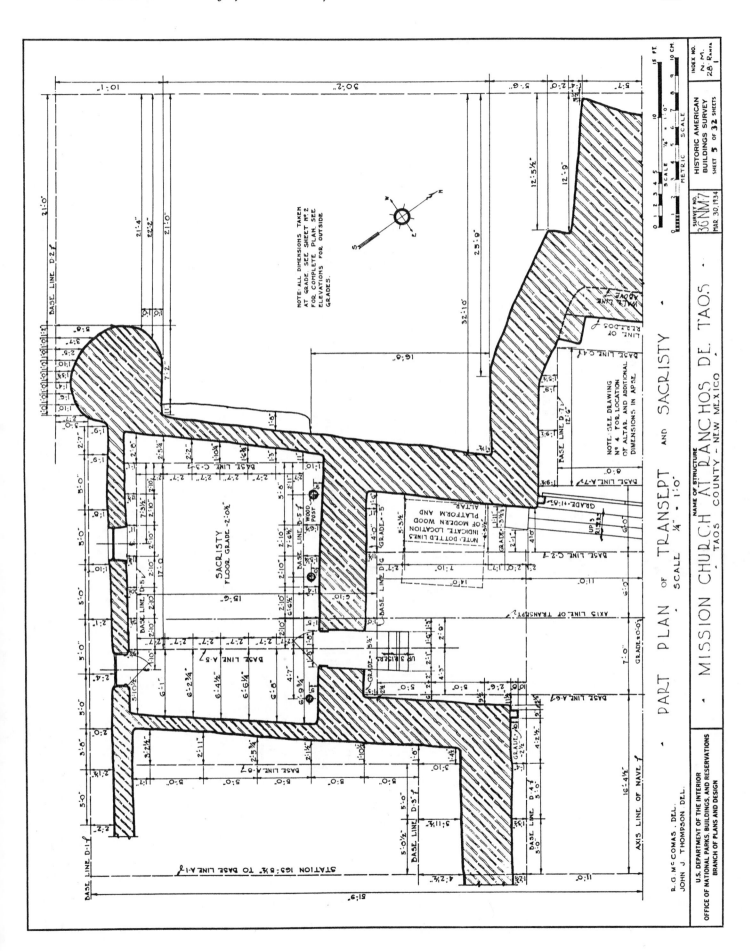

PART PLAN of TRANSEPT and SACRISTY

SCALE ¼" = 1'-0"

MISSION CHURCH AT RANCHOS DE TAOS

TAOS COUNTY · NEW MEXICO

R. G. McCOMAS. DEL.
JOHN J. THOMPSON DEL.

U.S. DEPARTMENT OF THE INTERIOR
OFFICE OF NATIONAL PARKS, BUILDINGS, AND RESERVATIONS
BRANCH OF PLANS AND DESIGN

SURVEY NO. 36 NM 77
MAR 30, 1934

HISTORIC AMERICAN
BUILDINGS SURVEY
SHEET 5 OF 32 SHEETS

INDEX NO.
N. M.
28 R-TA

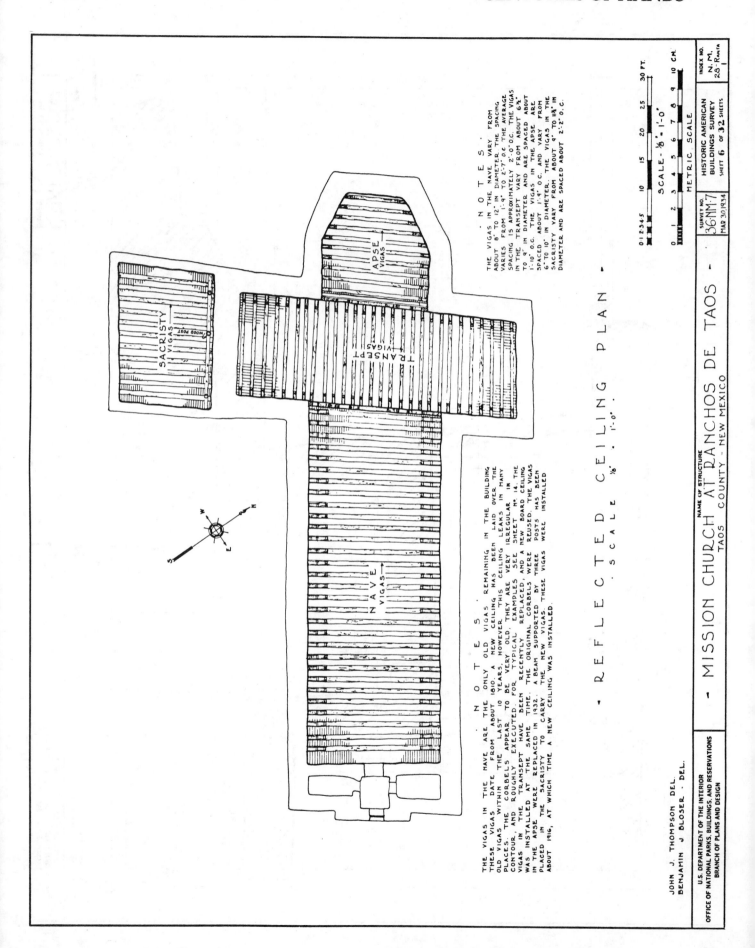

- REFLECTED CEILING PLAN -
- SCALE ⅛" = 1'-0" -

N O T E S .

THE VIGAS IN THE NAVE ARE THE ONLY OLD VIGAS REMAINING IN THE BUILDING THESE VIGAS DATE FROM ABOUT 1810. A NEW CEILING HAS BEEN LAID OVER THE OLD VIGAS WITHIN THE LAST 10 YEARS, HOWEVER, THIS CEILING LEAKS IN MANY PLACES. THE CORBELS APPEAR TO BE VERY OLD, THEY ARE VERY IRREGULAR IN CONTOUR, AND ROUGHLY EXECUTED FOR TYPICAL EXAMPLES, SEE SHEET Nº 14. THE VIGAS IN THE TRANSEPT HAVE BEEN RECENTLY REPLACED, AND A NEW BOARD CEILING WAS INSTALLED AT THE SAME TIME. THE ORIGINAL CORBELS WERE REUSED. THE VIGAS IN THE APSE WERE REPLACED IN 1932. A BEAM SUPPORTED BY THREE POSTS HAS BEEN PLACED IN THE SACRISTY TO CARRY THE NEW VIGAS. THESE VIGAS WERE INSTALLED ABOUT 1916, AT WHICH TIME A NEW CEILING WAS INSTALLED.

N O T E S .

THE VIGAS IN THE NAVE VARY FROM ABOUT 8" TO 12" IN DIAMETER. THE SPACING VARIES FROM 1'-9" TO 2'-7" O.C. THE AVERAGE SPACING IS APPROXIMATELY 2'-0" O.C. THE VIGAS IN THE TRANSEPT VARY FROM ABOUT 6¾" TO 9" IN DIAMETER AND ARE SPACED ABOUT 1'-10" O.C. THE VIGAS IN THE APSE. ARE SPACED ABOUT 1'-4" O.C. AND VARY FROM 6" TO 10" IN DIAMETER. THE VIGAS IN THE SACRISTY VARY FROM ABOUT 9" TO 11¾" IN DIAMETER AND ARE SPACED ABOUT 2'-2" O.C.

JOHN J. THOMPSON DEL.
BENJAMIN J BLOSER - DEL.

U.S. DEPARTMENT OF THE INTERIOR
OFFICE OF NATIONAL PARKS, BUILDINGS, AND RESERVATIONS
BRANCH OF PLANS AND DESIGN

NAME OF STRUCTURE
- MISSION CHURCH AT RANCHOS DE TAOS -
TAOS COUNTY - NEW MEXICO

SURVEY NO.
36-NM-7
MAR 30,1934

SCALE - ⅛" = 1'-0"
0 1 2 3 4 5    10    15    20    25    30 FT.

METRIC SCALE
0   1   2   3   4   5   6   7   8   9   10 CM.

HISTORIC AMERICAN
BUILDINGS SURVEY
SHEET 6 OF 32 SHEETS

INDEX. NO.
N. M.
28-RANTA
1

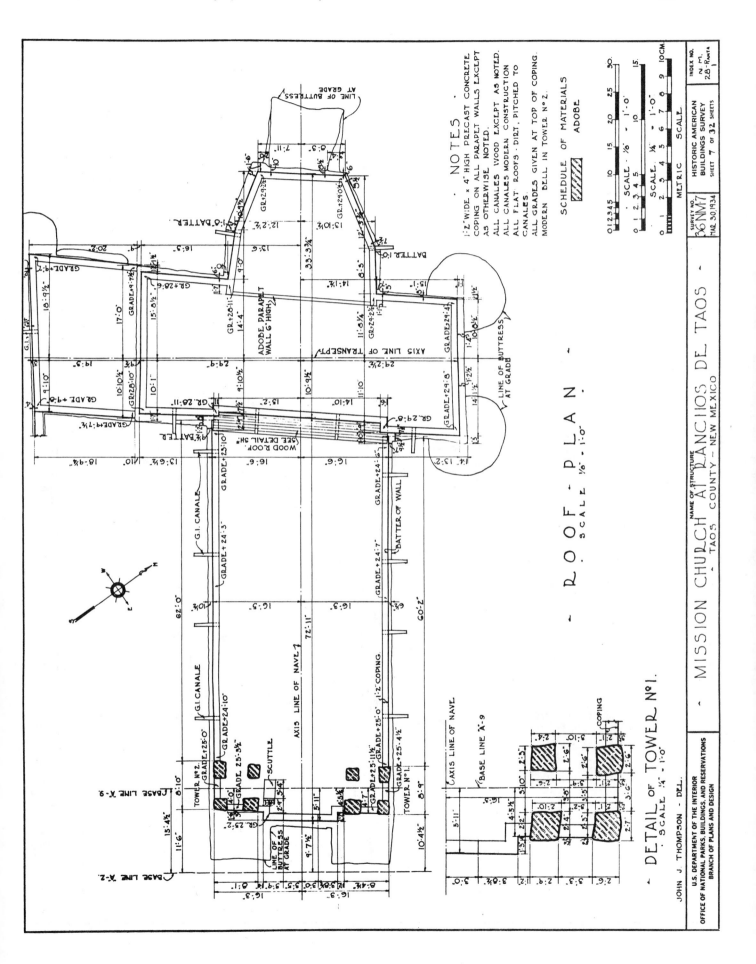

NOTES

1'2" WIDE x 4" HIGH PRECAST CONCRETE COPING ON ALL PARAPET WALLS EXCEPT AS OTHERWISE NOTED.
ALL CANALES WOOD EXCEPT AS NOTED.
ALL CANALES MODERN CONSTRUCTION
ALL FLAT ROOFS DIRT, PITCHED TO CANALES
ALL GRADES GIVEN AT TOP OF COPING.
MODERN BELL IN TOWER N°2.

SCHEDULE OF MATERIALS
ADOBE

- ROOF - PLAN -
SCALE ⅛" - 1'-0"

- DETAIL OF TOWER N°1. -
SCALE ¼" - 1'-0"

JOHN J. THOMPSON - DEL.

U.S. DEPARTMENT OF THE INTERIOR
OFFICE OF NATIONAL PARKS, BUILDINGS, AND RESERVATIONS
BRANCH OF PLANS AND DESIGN

MISSION CHURCH AT RANCHOS DE TAOS
- TAOS COUNTY - NEW MEXICO -

HISTORIC AMERICAN
BUILDINGS SURVEY
SHEET 7 OF 32 SHEETS

SURVEY NO. 36-NM-7
MAR 30, 1934

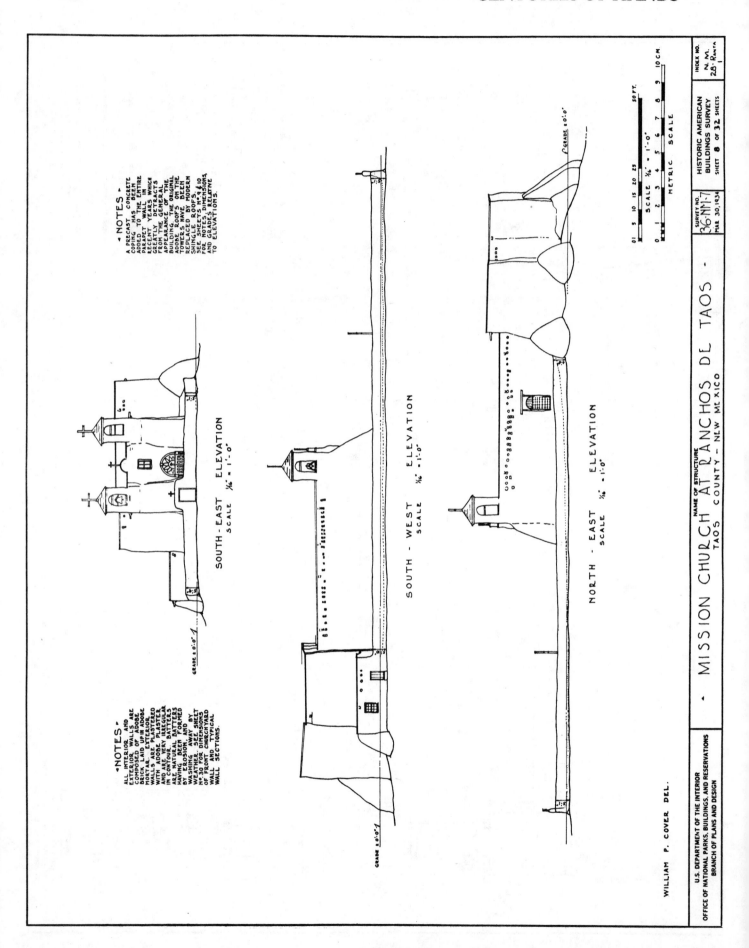

- NOTES -

A PRECAST CONCRETE COPING HAS BEEN ADDED TO THE ENTIRE PARAPET WALL IN RECENT YEARS WHICH GREATLY DETRACTS FROM THE GENERAL APPEARANCE OF THE BUILDING. THE ORIGINAL ADOBE ROOFS ON THE TOWERS HAVE BEEN REPLACED BY MODERN SHINGLE ROOFS. SEE SHEETS Nº 9 & 10 FOR NOTES, DIMENSIONS AND GRADES RELATIVE TO ELEVATIONS.

SOUTH - EAST   ELEVATION
SCALE  ⅛" = 1'-0"

SOUTH - WEST   ELEVATION
SCALE  ⅛" = 1'-0"

NORTH - EAST   ELEVATION
SCALE  ⅛" = 1'-0"

- NOTES -

ALL INTERIOR AND EXTERIOR WALLS ARE COMPOSED OF ADOBE BRICK LAID UP IN ADOBE MORTAR. EXTERIOR WALLS ARE PLASTERED WITH ADOBE PLASTER, AND ARE VERY IRREGULAR IN CONTOUR. BATTERS ARE NATURAL BATTERS HAVING BEEN FORMED BY EROSION, AND WASHING AWAY BY WEATHER. SEE SHEET Nº 30 FOR DIMENSIONS OF FRONT CHURCHYARD WALL AND TYPICAL WALL SECTIONS.

WILLIAM P. COVER DEL.

U.S. DEPARTMENT OF THE INTERIOR
OFFICE OF NATIONAL PARKS, BUILDINGS, AND RESERVATIONS
BRANCH OF PLANS AND DESIGN

MISSION CHURCH AT RANCHOS DE TAOS -
TAOS COUNTY - NEW MEXICO

SURVEY NO.
36 NM-7
MAR. 30,1934

HISTORIC AMERICAN
BUILDINGS SURVEY
SHEET 8 OF 32 SHEETS

INDEX NO.
N. M.
28-RnTA
1

SCALE  ⅛" = 1'-0"
METRIC SCALE

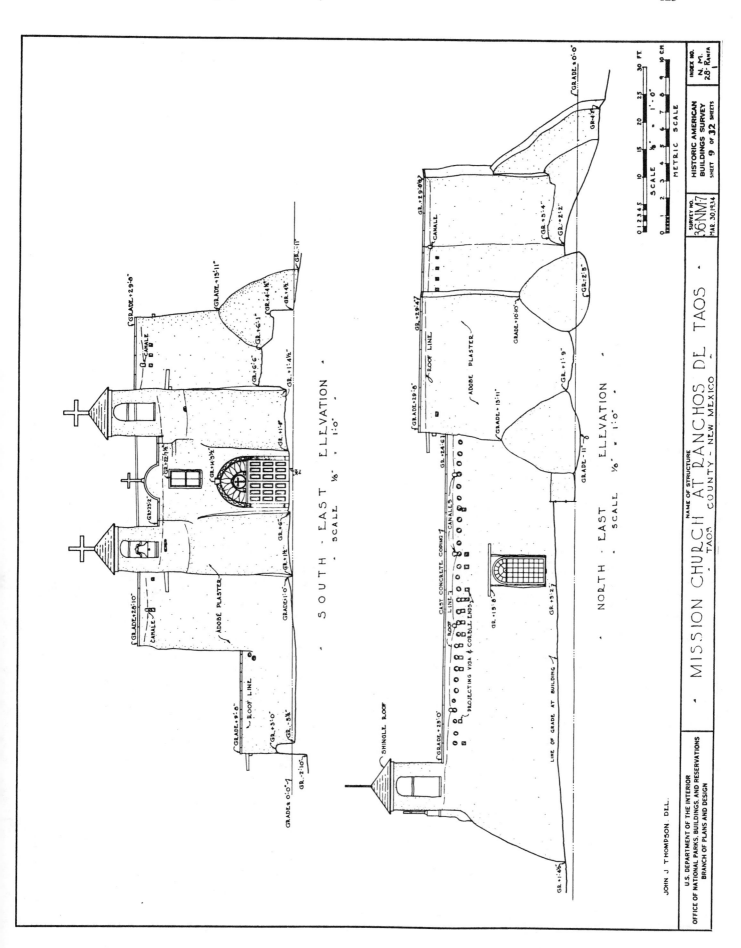

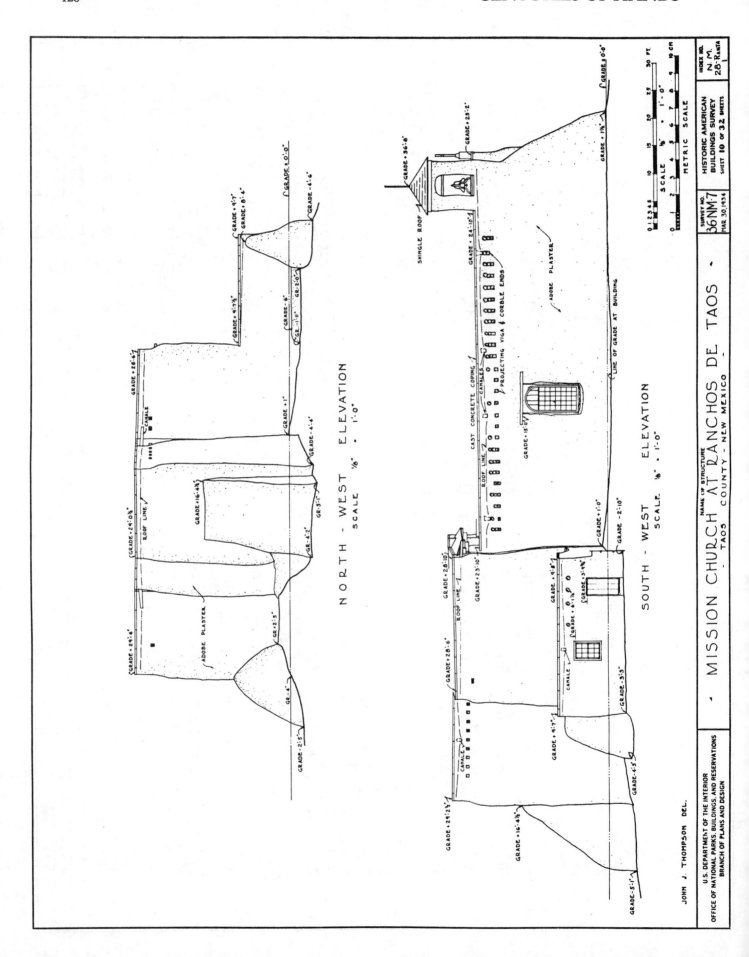

N O R T H - W E S T   E L E V A T I O N
SCALE ⅛" = 1'·0"

S O U T H - W E S T   E L E V A T I O N
SCALE ⅛" = 1'·0"

- MISSION CHURCH AT RANCHOS DE TAOS -
NAME OF STRUCTURE
- TAOS COUNTY - NEW MEXICO -

U.S. DEPARTMENT OF THE INTERIOR
OFFICE OF NATIONAL PARKS, BUILDINGS, AND RESERVATIONS
BRANCH OF PLANS AND DESIGN

JOHN J. THOMPSON   DEL.

SURVEY NO.
36NM7
MAR. 30, 1934

HISTORIC AMERICAN
BUILDINGS SURVEY
SHEET 10 OF 32 SHEETS

INDEX NO.
N. M.
28 RANCH

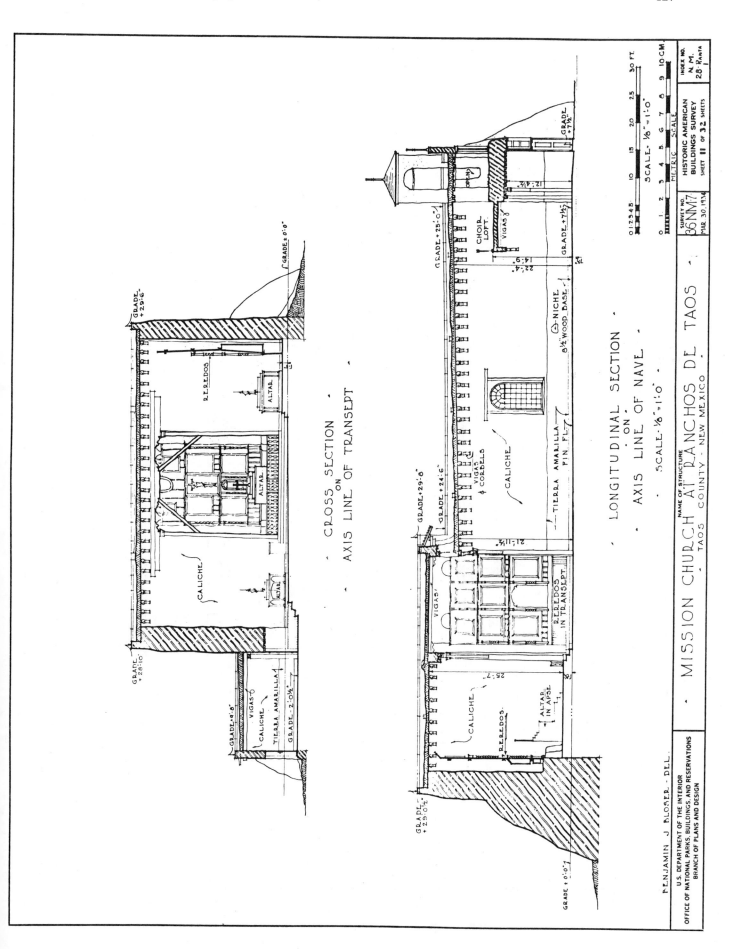

CROSS SECTION
ON
AXIS LINE OF TRANSEPT

LONGITUDINAL SECTION
ON
AXIS LINE OF NAVE

SCALE ⅛" = 1'-0"

MISSION CHURCH AT RANCHOS DE TAOS
TAOS COUNTY · NEW MEXICO

BENJAMIN J. BLOSER - DEL.

U.S. DEPARTMENT OF THE INTERIOR
OFFICE OF NATIONAL PARKS, BUILDINGS, AND RESERVATIONS
BRANCH OF PLANS AND DESIGN

SURVEY NO. 36 NM 17
MAR. 30, 1934

HISTORIC AMERICAN
BUILDINGS SURVEY
SHEET 11 OF 32 SHEETS

INDEX NO.
N.M.
28-Ranta
1

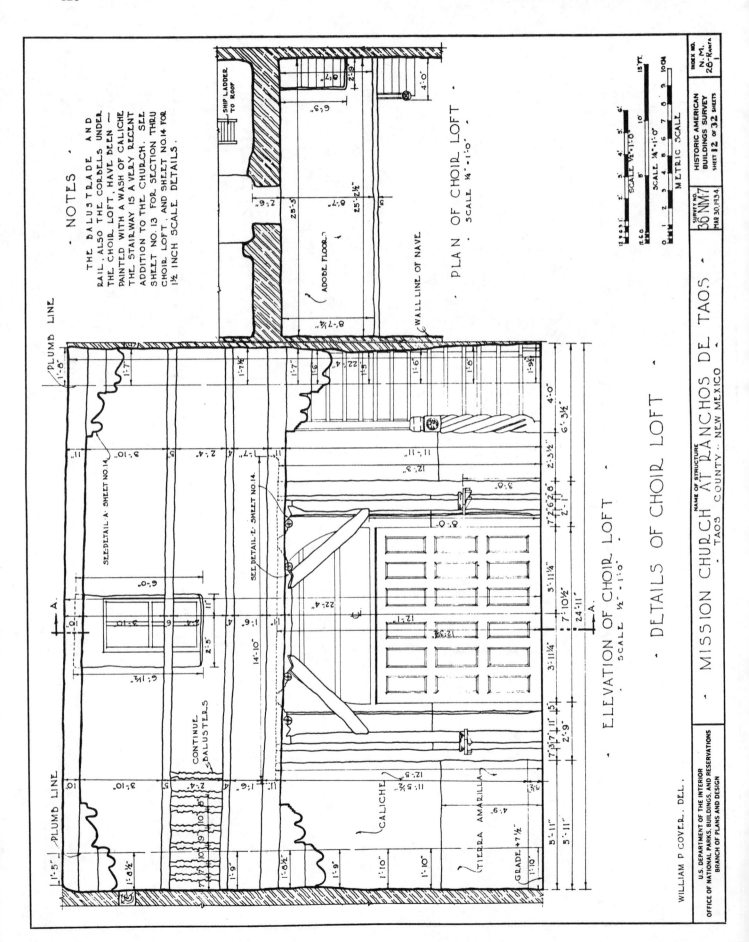

- DETAILS OF CHOIR LOFT -

- ELEVATION OF CHOIR LOFT -
SCALE ½" = 1'-0"

- PLAN OF CHOIR LOFT -
SCALE ¼" = 1'-0"

- NOTES -

THE BALUSTRADE AND RAIL, ALSO THE CORBELS UNDER THE CHOIR LOFT, HAVE BEEN PAINTED WITH A WASH OF CALICHE THE STAIRWAY IS A VERY RECENT ADDITION TO THE CHURCH. SEE SHEET NO. 13 FOR SECTION THRU CHOIR LOFT, AND SHEET NO. 14 FOR 1½ INCH SCALE DETAILS.

MISSION CHURCH AT RANCHOS DE TAOS.
- TAOS COUNTY - NEW MEXICO -

WILLIAM P. COVER. DEL.

U.S. DEPARTMENT OF THE INTERIOR
OFFICE OF NATIONAL PARKS, BUILDINGS, AND RESERVATIONS
BRANCH OF PLANS AND DESIGN

HISTORIC AMERICAN BUILDINGS SURVEY
SHEET 12 OF 32 SHEETS

INDEX NO.
N. M.
28-RANFA

SURVEY NO.
36 NM 7
MAR 30, 1934

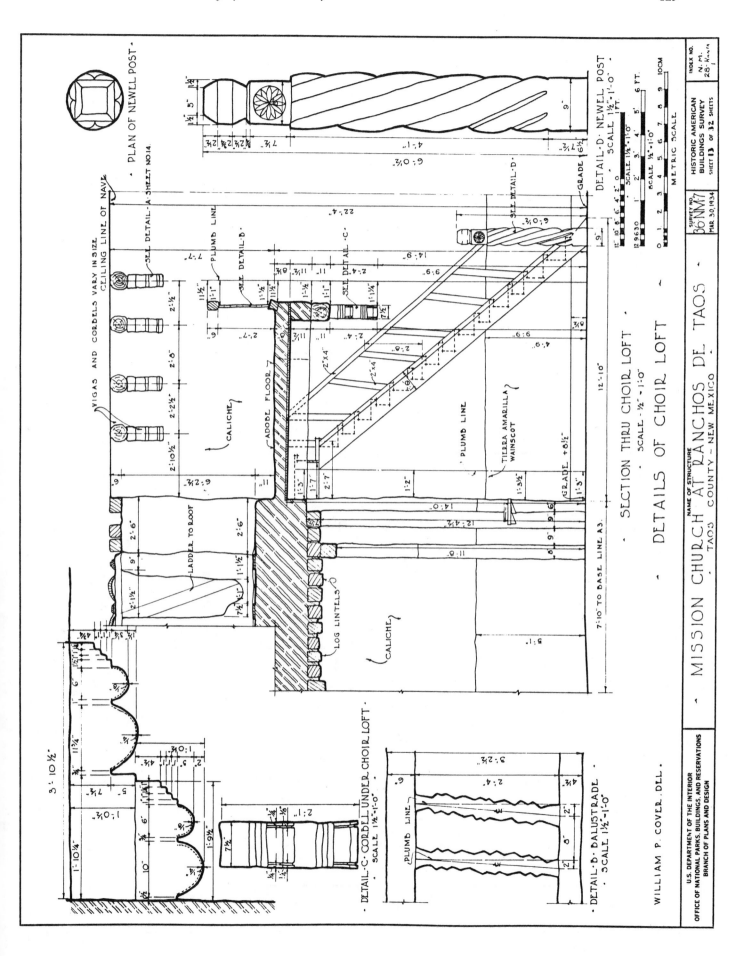

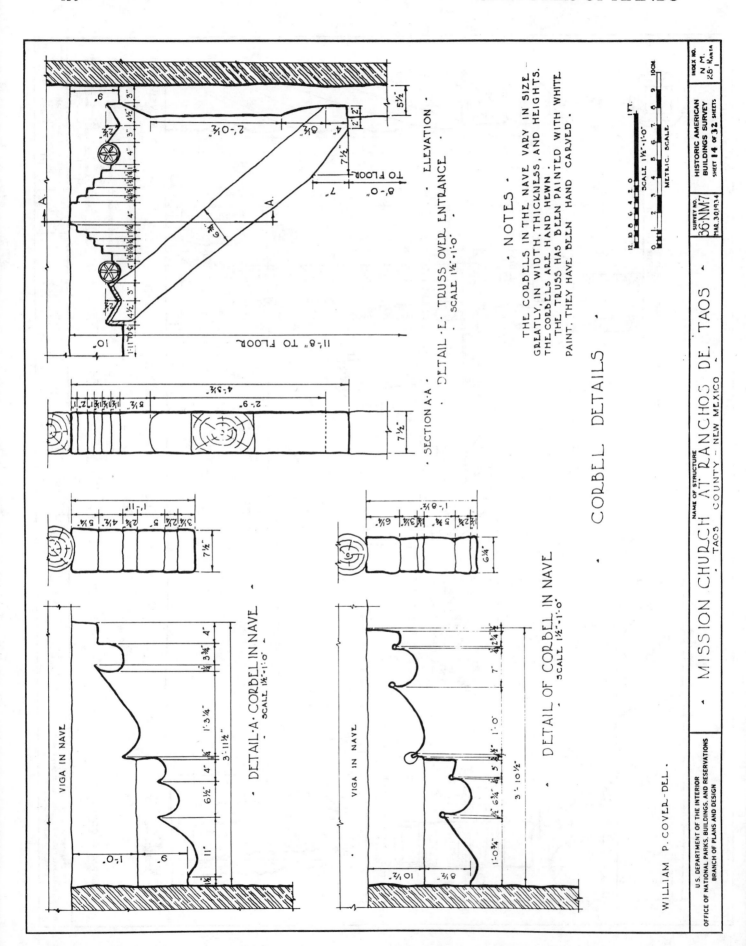

· DETAIL · E · TRUSS OVER ENTRANCE ·
SCALE 1½"=1'-0"

· ELEVATION ·

· SECTION A-A ·

· NOTES ·

THE CORBELS IN THE NAVE VARY IN SIZE GREATLY, IN WIDTH, THICKNESS, AND HEIGHTS. THE CORBELS ARE HAND HEWN. THE TRUSS HAS BEEN PAINTED WITH WHITE PAINT. THEY HAVE BEEN HAND CARVED.

· DETAIL · A · CORBEL IN NAVE ·
SCALE 1½"=1'-0"

VIGA IN NAVE

DETAIL OF CORBEL IN NAVE
SCALE 1½"=1'-0"

VIGA IN NAVE

· CORBEL DETAILS ·

WILLIAM P. COVER - DEL.

U.S. DEPARTMENT OF THE INTERIOR
OFFICE OF NATIONAL PARKS, BUILDINGS, AND RESERVATIONS
BRANCH OF PLANS AND DESIGN

NAME OF STRUCTURE
· MISSION CHURCH AT RANCHOS DE. TAOS ·
· TAOS COUNTY - NEW MEXICO ·

SURVEY NO.
36·NM·7
MAR. 30, 1934

HISTORIC AMERICAN
BUILDINGS SURVEY
SHEET 14 OF 32 SHEETS

INDEX NO.
N. M.
28·KANTA
1

SCALE 1½"=1'-0"
METRIC. SCALE

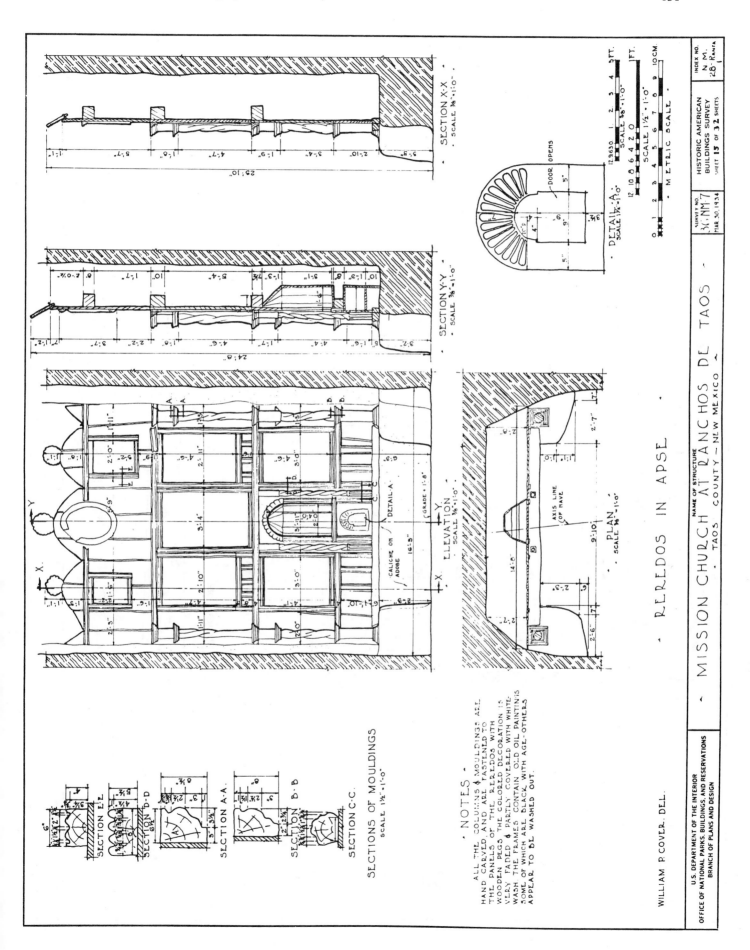

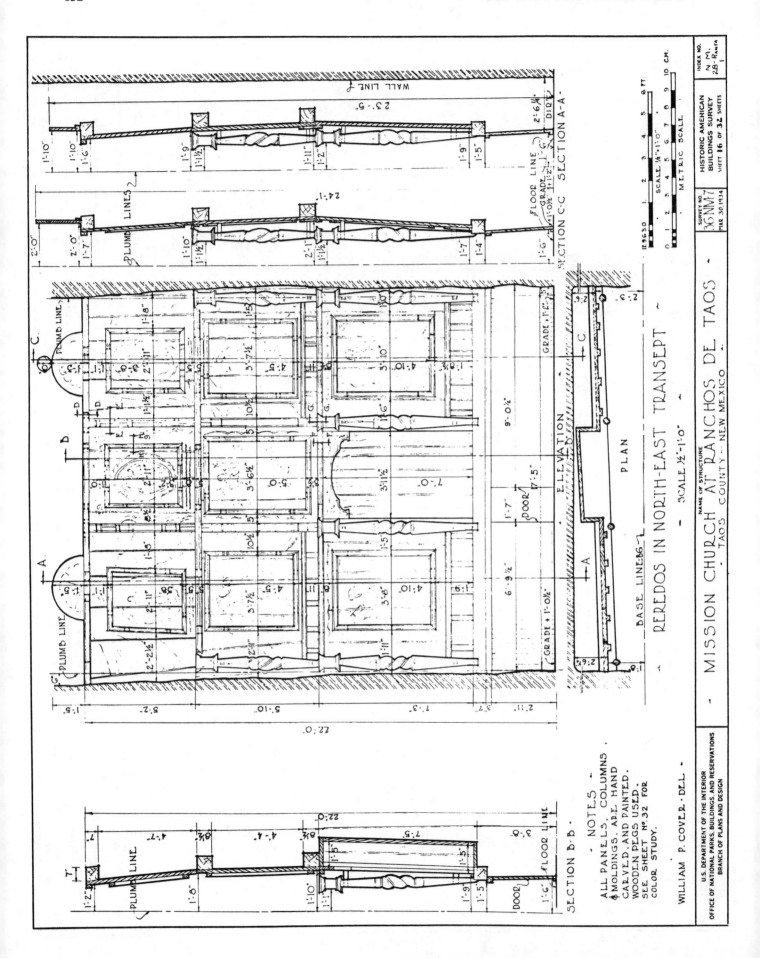

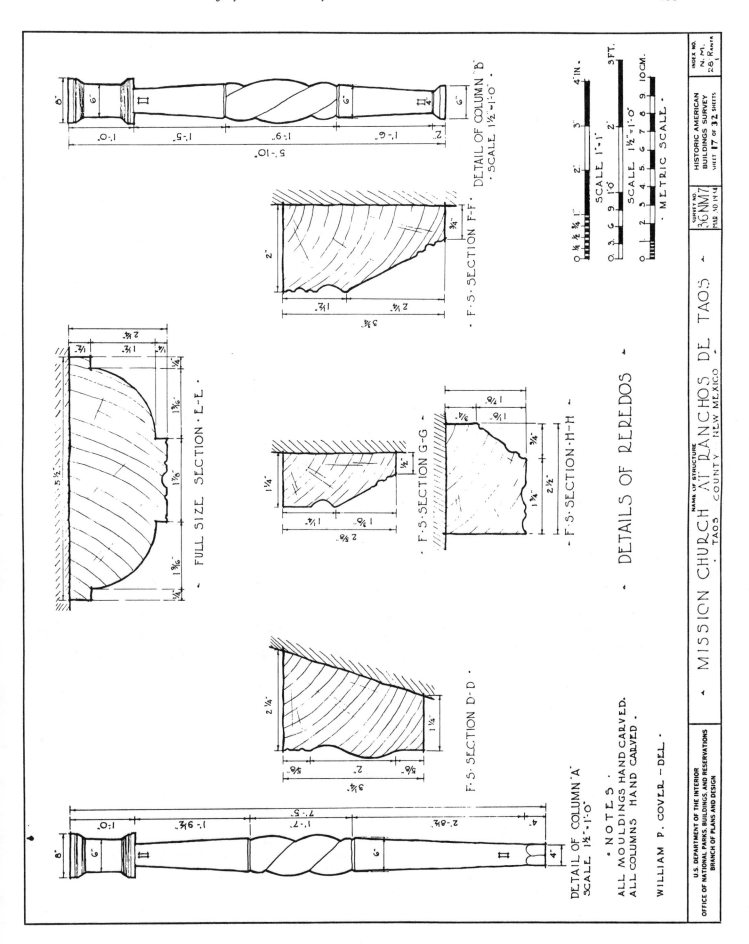

DETAILS OF REREDOS

MISSION CHURCH AT RANCHOS DE TAOS
· TAOS COUNTY · NEW MEXICO ·

· NOTES ·
ALL MOULDINGS HAND CARVED.
ALL COLUMNS HAND CARVED.

WILLIAM P. COVER – DEL ·

U.S. DEPARTMENT OF THE INTERIOR
OFFICE OF NATIONAL PARKS, BUILDINGS, AND RESERVATIONS
BRANCH OF PLANS AND DESIGN

NAME OF STRUCTURE

SURVEY NO. 36 NM 7
MAR. 30 1934

INDEX NO.
N. M.
28 RANCH

HISTORIC AMERICAN
BUILDINGS SURVEY
SHEET 17 OF 32 SHEETS

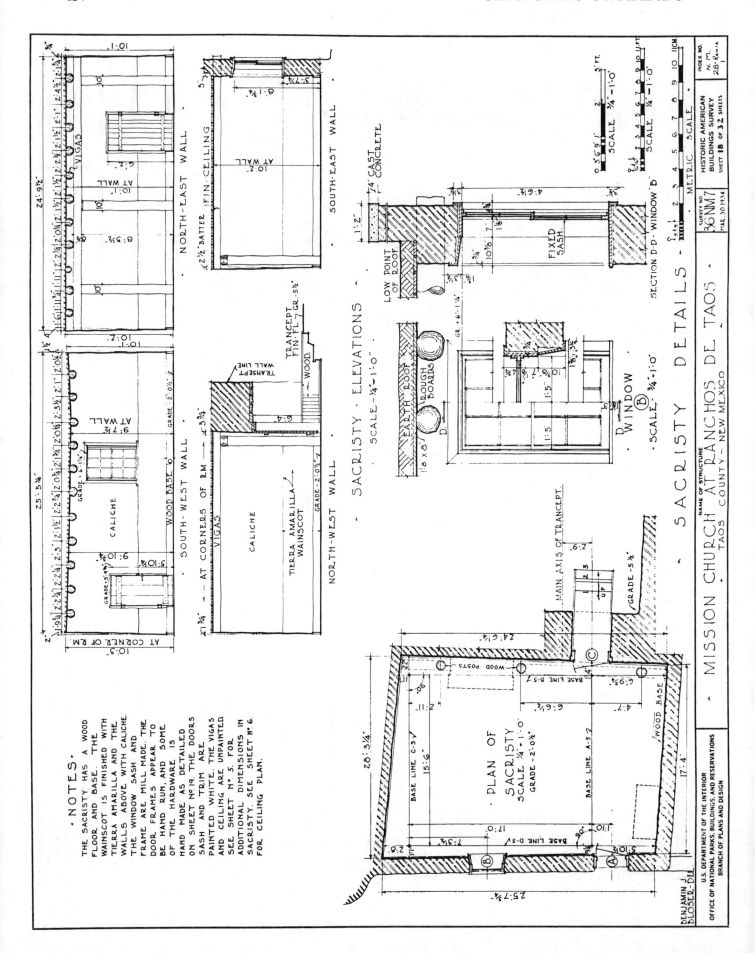

· NOTES ·

THE SACRISTY HAS A WOOD
FLOOR AND BASE. THE
WAINSCOT IS FINISHED WITH
TIERRA AMARILLA AND THE
WALLS ABOVE WITH CALICHE.
THE WINDOW SASH AND
FRAME ARE MILL MADE. THE
DOOR FRAMES APPEAR TO
BE HAND RUN, AND SOME
OF THE HARDWARE IS
HAND MADE AS DETAILED
ON SHEET Nº 19. THE DOORS
SASH AND TRIM ARE
PAINTED WHITE. THE VIGAS
AND CEILING ARE UNPAINTED
SEE SHEET Nº 5. FOR
ADDITIONAL DIMENSIONS IN
SACRISTY. SEE SHEET Nº 6.
FOR CEILING PLAN.

· SACRISTY · ELEVATIONS ·
SCALE ¼"-1'0"

· PLAN OF SACRISTY ·
SCALE ¼"-1'0"

· SACRISTY DETAILS ·

NORTH-EAST WALL

SOUTH-EAST WALL

SOUTH-WEST WALL

NORTH-WEST WALL

· MISSION CHURCH AT RANCHOS DE TAOS ·
TAOS COUNTY · NEW MEXICO

BENJAMIN J. BLOSSER, DEL.

U.S. DEPARTMENT OF THE INTERIOR
OFFICE OF NATIONAL PARKS, BUILDINGS, AND RESERVATIONS
BRANCH OF PLANS AND DESIGN

HISTORIC AMERICAN
BUILDINGS SURVEY
SHEET 18 OF 32 SHEETS

INDEX NO.
N. M.
28-RANTA
1

SURVEY NO
36 NM 7
MAR. 30 1934

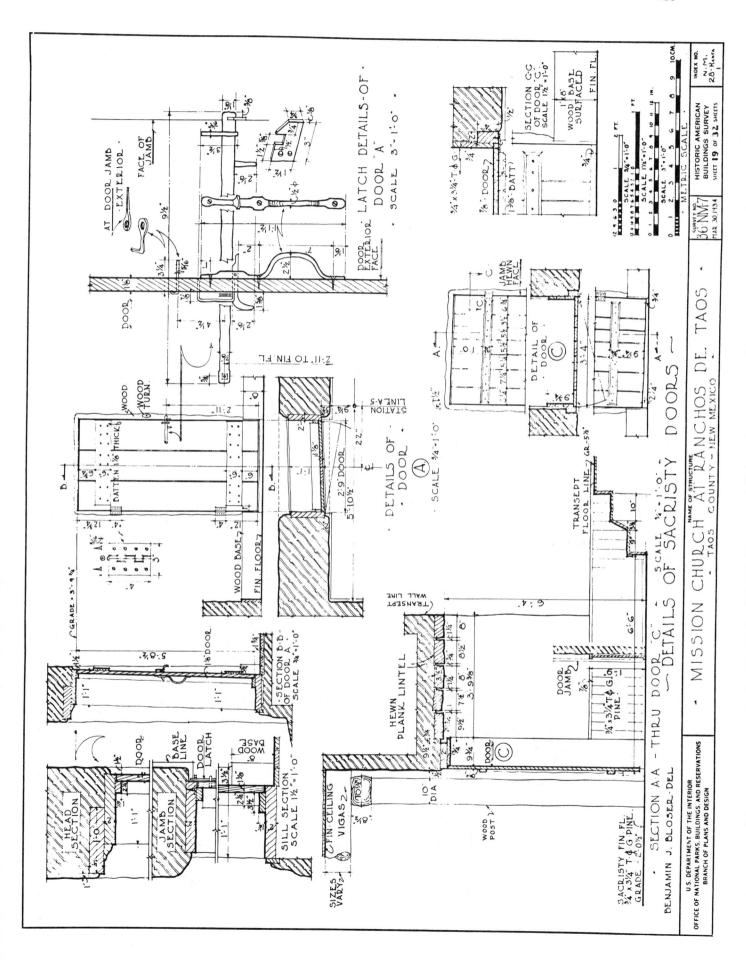

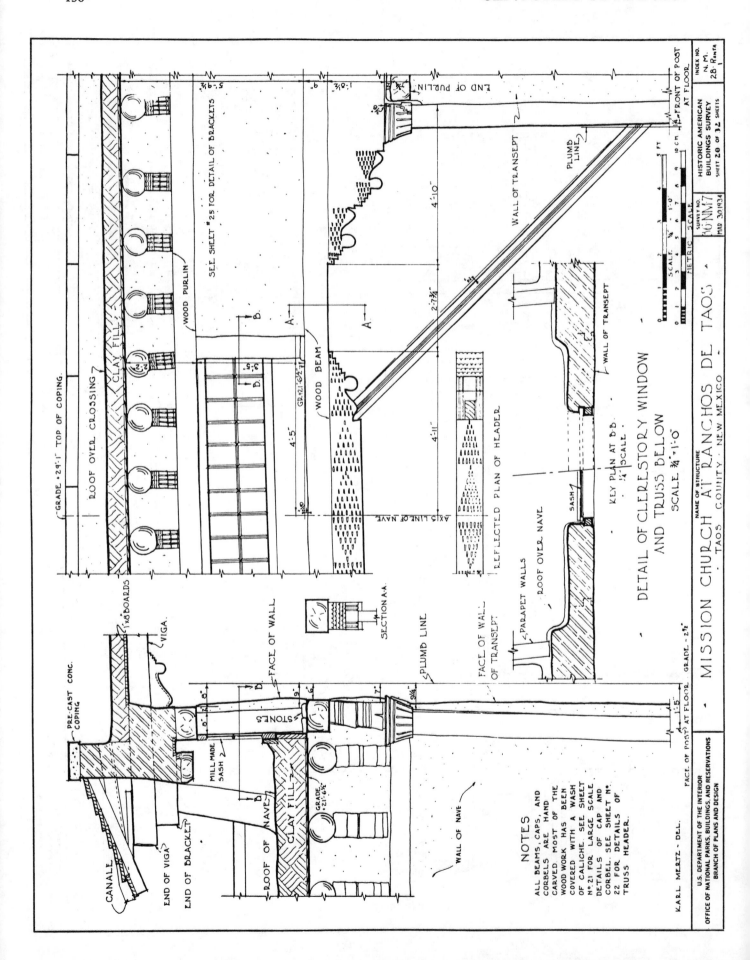

NOTES

ALL BEAMS, CAPS, AND CORBELS ARE HAND CARVED MOST OF THE WOOD WORK HAS BEEN COVERED WITH A WASH OF CALICHE. SEE SHEET Nº 21 FOR LARGE SCALE DETAILS OF CAP AND CORBEL. SEE SHEET Nº 22 FOR DETAILS OF TRUSS HEADER.

DETAIL OF CLERESTORY WINDOW AND TRUSS BELOW
SCALE ¾"=1'-0"

MISSION CHURCH AT RANCHOS DE TAOS
TAOS COUNTY NEW MEXICO

U.S. DEPARTMENT OF THE INTERIOR
OFFICE OF NATIONAL PARKS, BUILDINGS, AND RESERVATIONS
BRANCH OF PLANS AND DESIGN

KARL MERTZ - DEL.

HISTORIC AMERICAN BUILDINGS SURVEY
SHEET 20 OF 32 SHEETS

INDEX NO.
N. M.
28. Ranta
1

SURVEY NO.
10 NM 17
MAR 30 1934

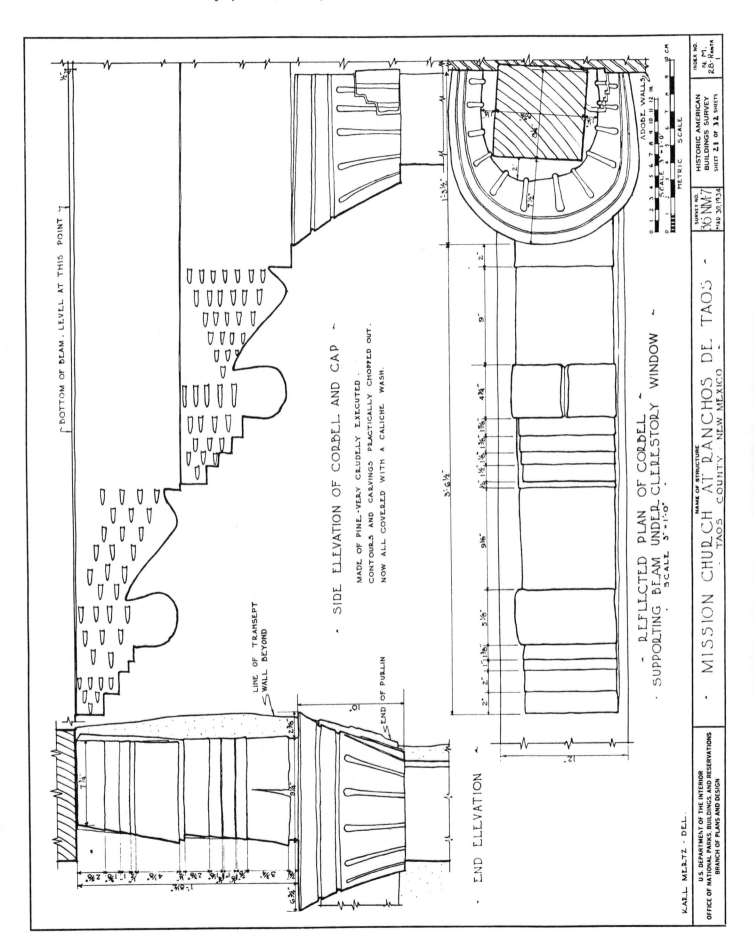

SIDE ELEVATION OF CORBEL AND CAP

MADE OF PINE - VERY CRUDELY EXECUTED.
CONTOURS AND CARVINGS PRACTICALLY CHOPPED OUT.
NOW ALL COVERED WITH A CALICHE WASH.

REFLECTED PLAN OF CORBEL
SUPPORTING BEAM UNDER CLERESTORY WINDOW
SCALE 3" = 1'-0"

END ELEVATION

KARL MERTZ - DEL.

U.S. DEPARTMENT OF THE INTERIOR
OFFICE OF NATIONAL PARKS, BUILDINGS, AND RESERVATIONS
BRANCH OF PLANS AND DESIGN

MISSION CHURCH AT RANCHOS DE TAOS
TAOS COUNTY · NEW MEXICO

SURVEY NO. 36 NM 7
MAD 30, 1934

HISTORIC AMERICAN
BUILDINGS SURVEY
SHEET 21 OF 32 SHEETS

INDEX NO.
N. M.
28 - RANTA
1

BOTTOM OF BEAM. LEVEL AT THIS POINT

LINE OF TRANSEPT
WALL BEYOND

END OF PURLIN

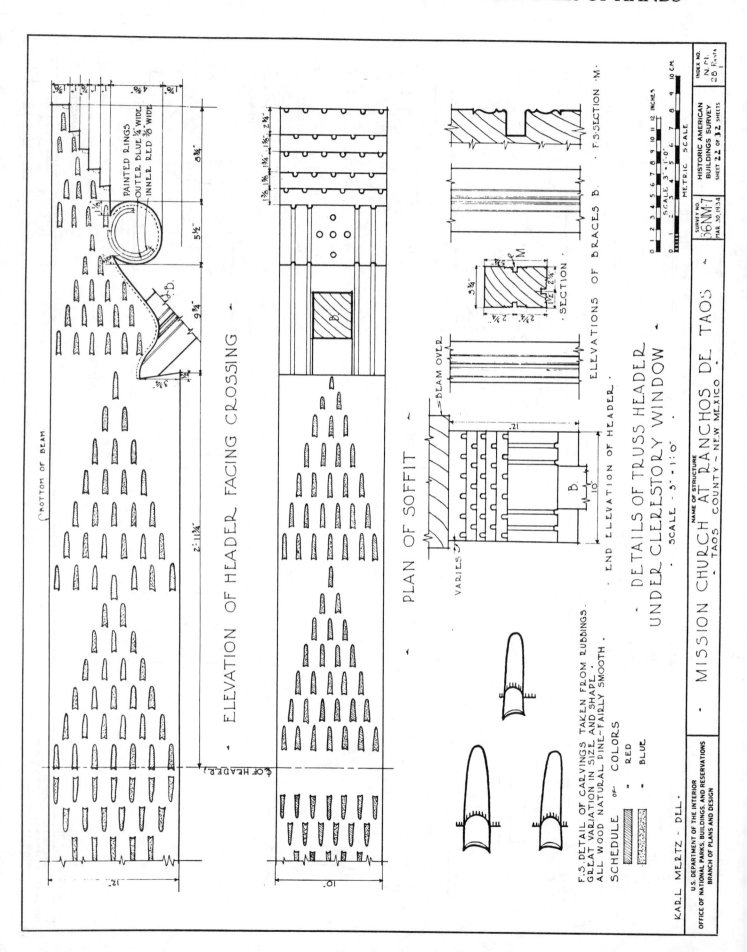

· ELEVATION OF HEADER FACING CROSSING ·

PAINTED RINGS
OUTER BLUE ¼ WIDE
INNER RED ⅜ WIDE

BOTTOM OF BEAM

¢ OF HEADER

· PLAN OF SOFFIT ·

VARIES

BEAM OVER

· END ELEVATION OF HEADER ·

· F.S. SECTION ·M·

· SECTION ·

· ELEVATIONS OF BRACES ·B·

F.S. DETAIL OF CARVINGS TAKEN FROM RUBBINGS.
GREAT VARIATION IN SIZE AND SHAPE.
ALL WOOD NATURAL PINE-FAIRLY SMOOTH.

SCHEDULE OF COLORS

⬛ = RED

▨ = BLUE

· DETAILS OF TRUSS HEADER
UNDER CLERESTORY WINDOW ·

· SCALE - 3" = 1'-0" ·

KARL MERTZ - DEL.

· MISSION CHURCH AT RANCHOS DE TAOS ·
· TAOS COUNTY - NEW MEXICO ·

U.S. DEPARTMENT OF THE INTERIOR
OFFICE OF NATIONAL PARKS, BUILDINGS, AND RESERVATIONS
BRANCH OF PLANS AND DESIGN

NAME OF STRUCTURE

SURVEY NO
36NM7
MAR.30,1934

HISTORIC AMERICAN
BUILDINGS SURVEY
SHEET 22 OF 32 SHEETS

INDEX NO.
N.M.
28 R.M.A.

SCALE 3" = 1'-0"

METRIC SCALE

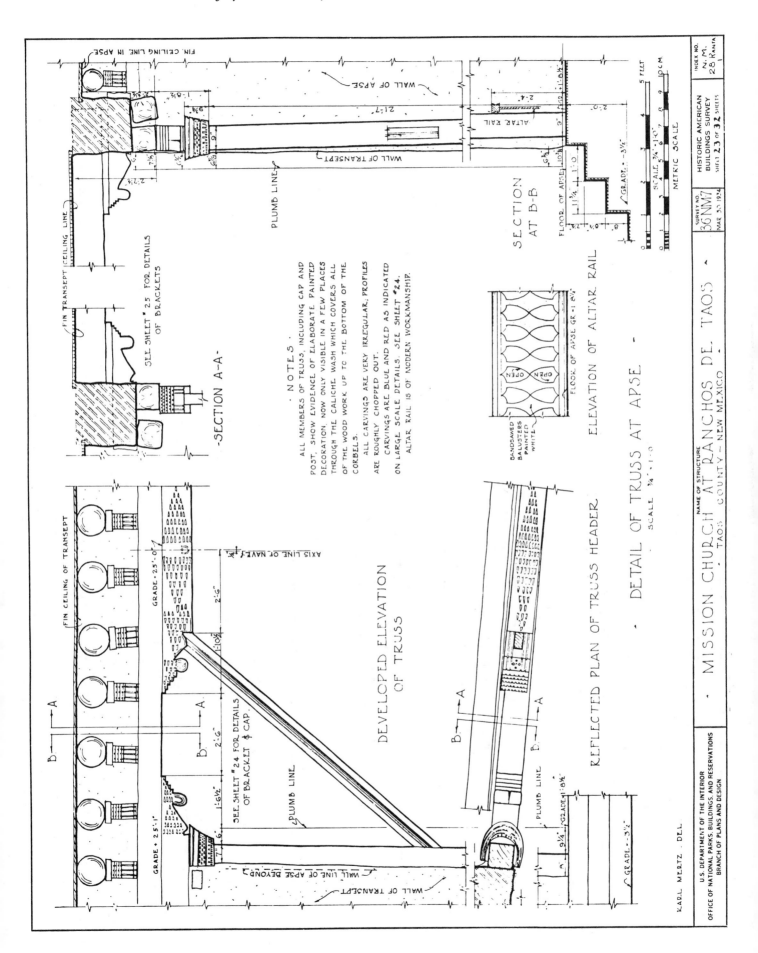

- SECTION A-A -

SECTION AT B-B

ELEVATION OF ALTAR RAIL

- DETAIL OF TRUSS AT APSE -

DEVELOPED ELEVATION OF TRUSS

REFLECTED PLAN OF TRUSS HEADER

· NOTES ·

ALL MEMBERS OF TRUSS, INCLUDING CAP AND POST, SHOW EVIDENCE OF ELABORATE PAINTED DECORATION NOW ONLY VISIBLE IN A FEW PLACES THROUGH THE CALICHE WASH WHICH COVERS ALL OF THE WOOD WORK UP TO THE BOTTOM OF THE CORBELS.

ALL CARVINGS ARE VERY IRREGULAR, PROFILES ARE ROUGHLY CHOPPED OUT.

CARVINGS ARE BLUE AND RED AS INDICATED ON LARGE SCALE DETAILS. SEE SHEET #24. ALTAR RAIL IS OF MODERN WORKMANSHIP.

MISSION CHURCH AT RANCHOS DE. TAOS ·
· TAOS COUNTY — NEW MEXICO ·

HISTORIC AMERICAN BUILDINGS SURVEY
SHEET 23 OF 32 SHEETS

U.S. DEPARTMENT OF THE INTERIOR
OFFICE OF NATIONAL PARKS, BUILDINGS, AND RESERVATIONS
BRANCH OF PLANS AND DESIGN

INDEX NO. N.M. 28 RANTA

SURVEY NO. 36 NM7
MAR 30 1934

KARL MERTZ . DEL.

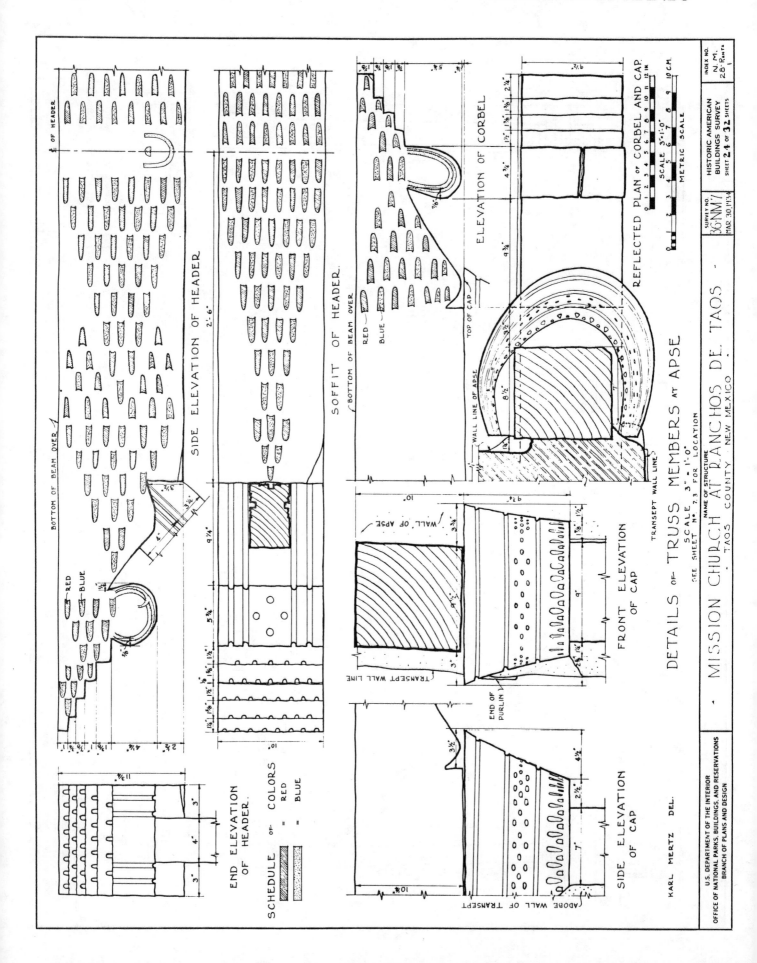

SIDE ELEVATION OF HEADER.
2'-6"

END ELEVATION OF HEADER.

SCHEDULE OF COLORS
= RED
= BLUE

SOFFIT OF HEADER.

BOTTOM OF BEAM OVER

ELEVATION OF CORBEL

REFLECTED PLAN OF CORBEL AND CAP.
SCALE 3"=1'-0"
METRIC SCALE

FRONT ELEVATION OF CAP

SIDE ELEVATION OF CAP

TRANSEPT WALL LINE

WALL OF APSE

WALL LINE OF APSE

END OF PURLIN

ADOBE WALL OF TRANSEPT

DETAILS OF TRUSS MEMBERS AT APSE
SCALE 3"=1'-0"
SEE SHEET N° 7.3 FOR LOCATION.

MISSION CHURCH AT RANCHOS DE TAOS -
TAOS COUNTY NEW MEXICO -

KARL MERTZ DEL.

U.S. DEPARTMENT OF THE INTERIOR
OFFICE OF NATIONAL PARKS, BUILDINGS, AND RESERVATIONS
BRANCH OF PLANS AND DESIGN

HISTORIC AMERICAN
BUILDINGS SURVEY
SHEET 24 OF 32 SHEETS

SURVEY N°
36-NM-1
MAR 30, 1934

INDEX NO.
N. M.
28 R·M·T·s
1

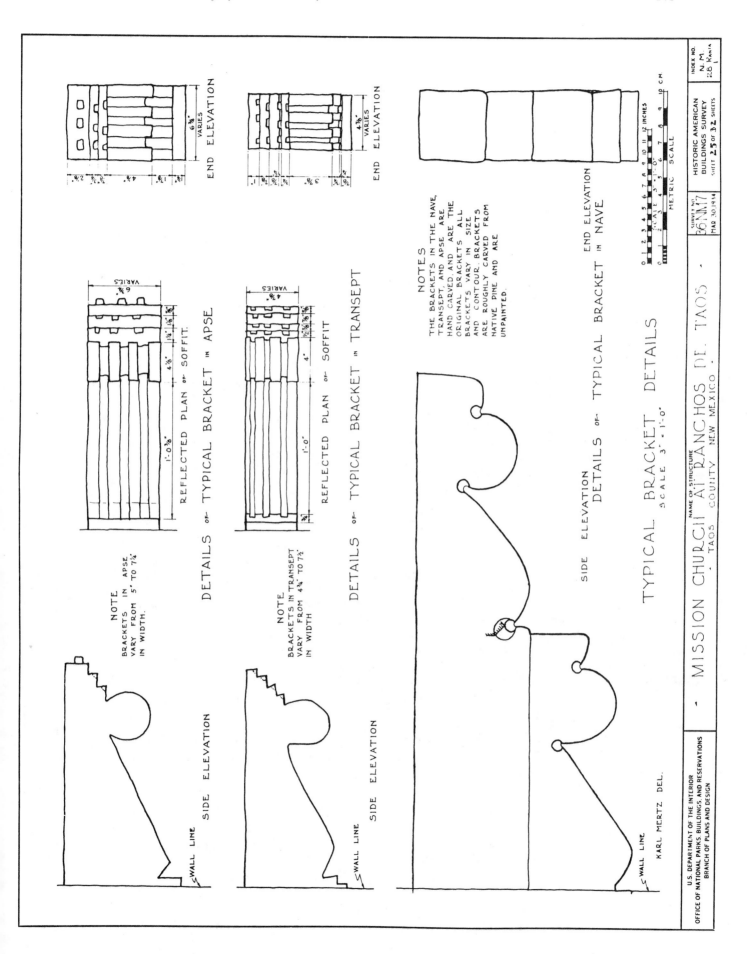

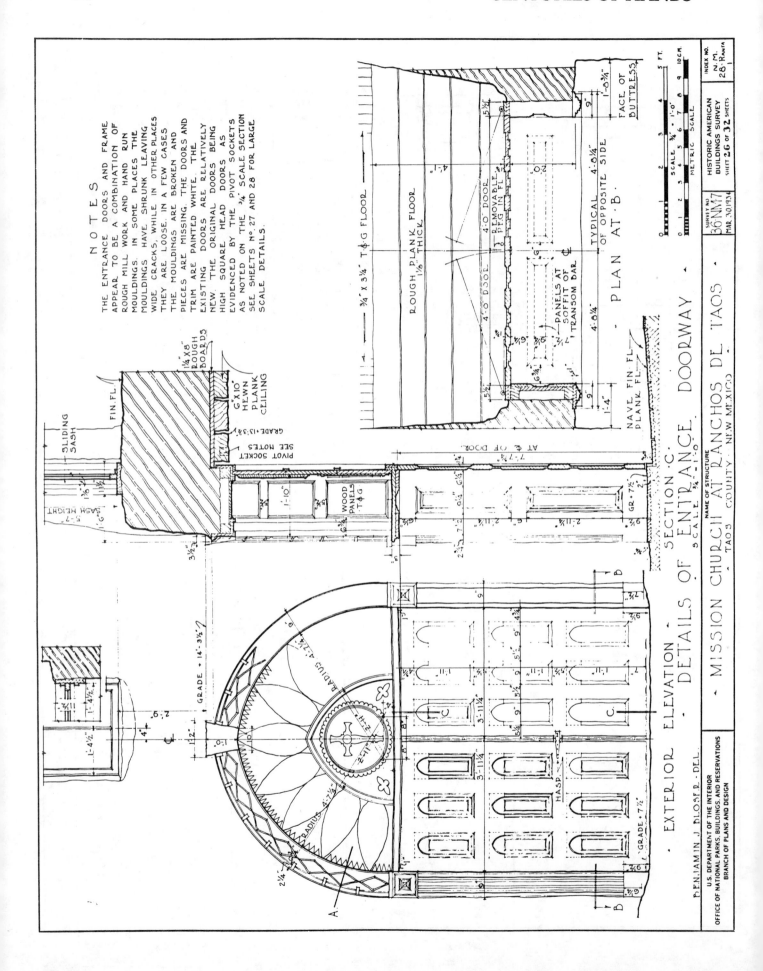

U.S. DEPARTMENT OF THE INTERIOR
OFFICE OF NATIONAL PARKS. BUILDINGS. AND RESERVATIONS
BRANCH OF PLANS AND DESIGN

HISTORIC AMERICAN
BUILDINGS SURVEY
SHEET 26 OF 32 SHEETS

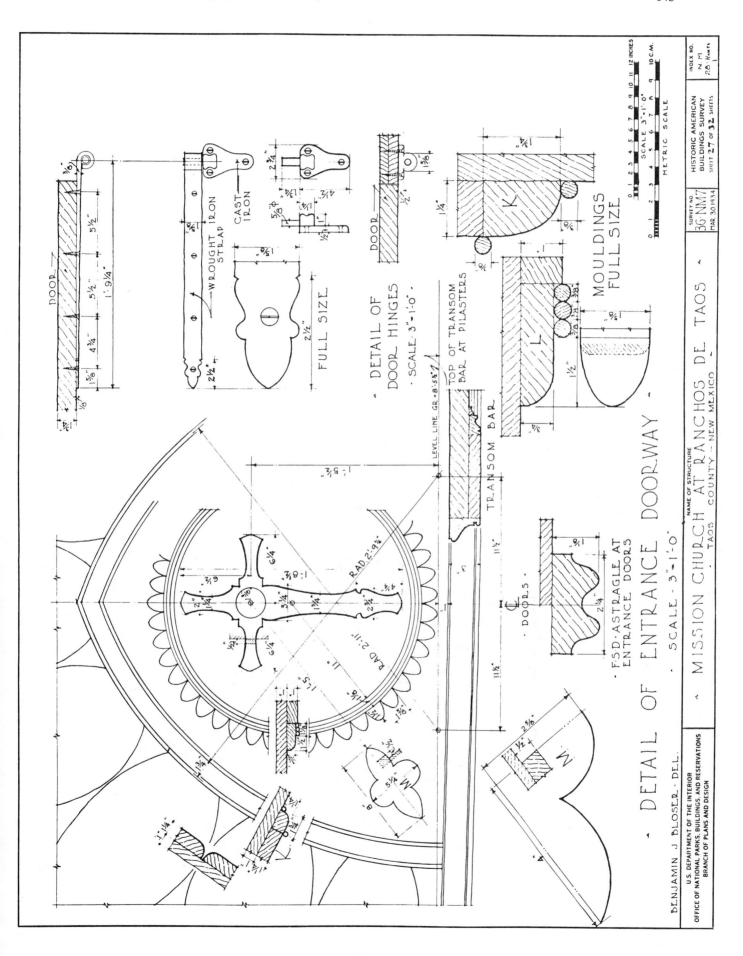

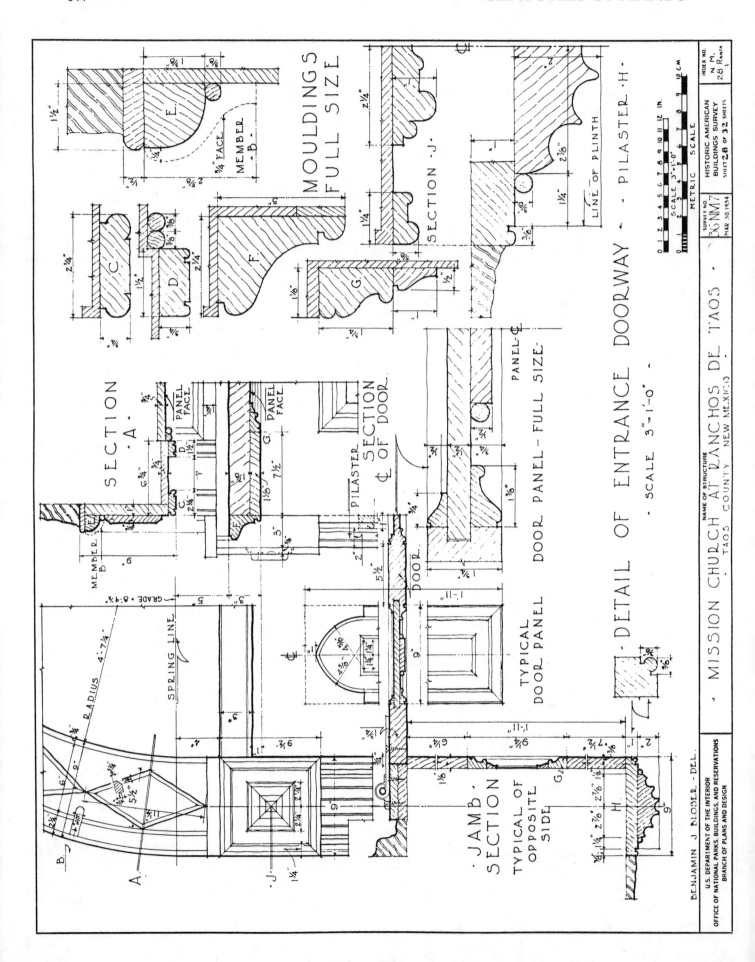

MOULDINGS FULL SIZE

SECTION · A ·

· JAMB · SECTION

TYPICAL DOOR PANEL

TYPICAL OF OPPOSITE SIDE

SECTION · J ·

SECTION ℄ OF DOOR

DOOR PANEL — FULL SIZE —

· DETAIL OF ENTRANCE DOORWAY · · PILASTER · H ·

· SCALE 3″ = 1′-0″ ·

BENJAMIN J. RLOSER · DEL.

U.S. DEPARTMENT OF THE INTERIOR
OFFICE OF NATIONAL PARKS, BUILDINGS, AND RESERVATIONS
BRANCH OF PLANS AND DESIGN

NAME OF STRUCTURE
· MISSION CHURCH AT RANCHOS DE TAOS ·
· TAOS COUNTY · NEW MEXICO ·

METRIC SCALE

SCALE 3″=1′-0″

HISTORIC AMERICAN
BUILDINGS SURVEY
SHEET 28 of 32 SHEETS

SURVEY NO.
36 NM7

MAR 30 1934

INDEX NO.
N. M.
28 RANIA

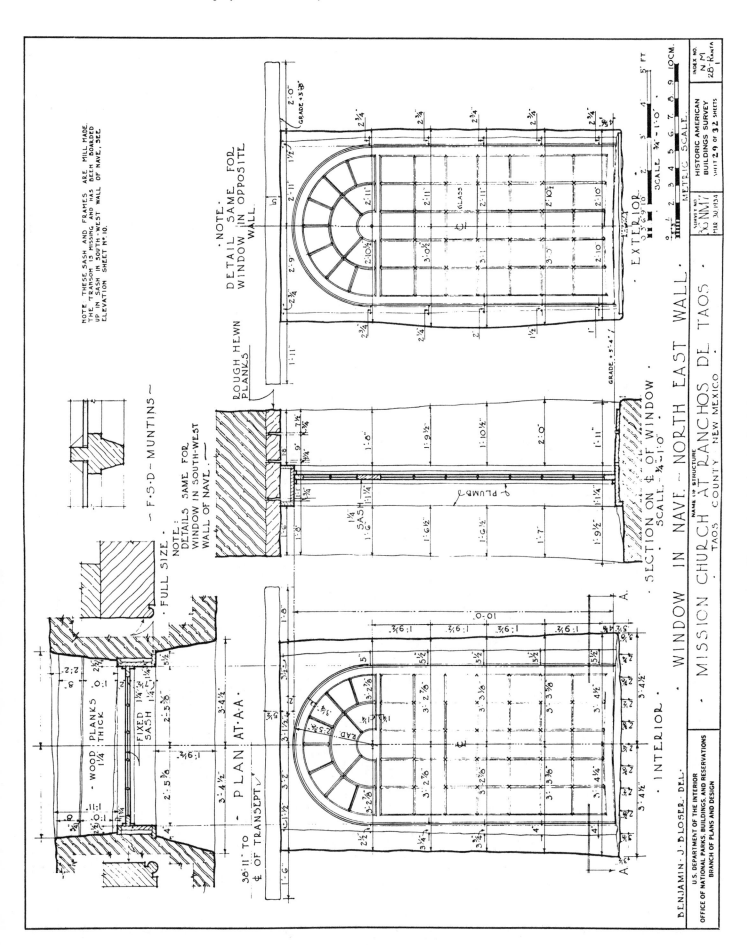

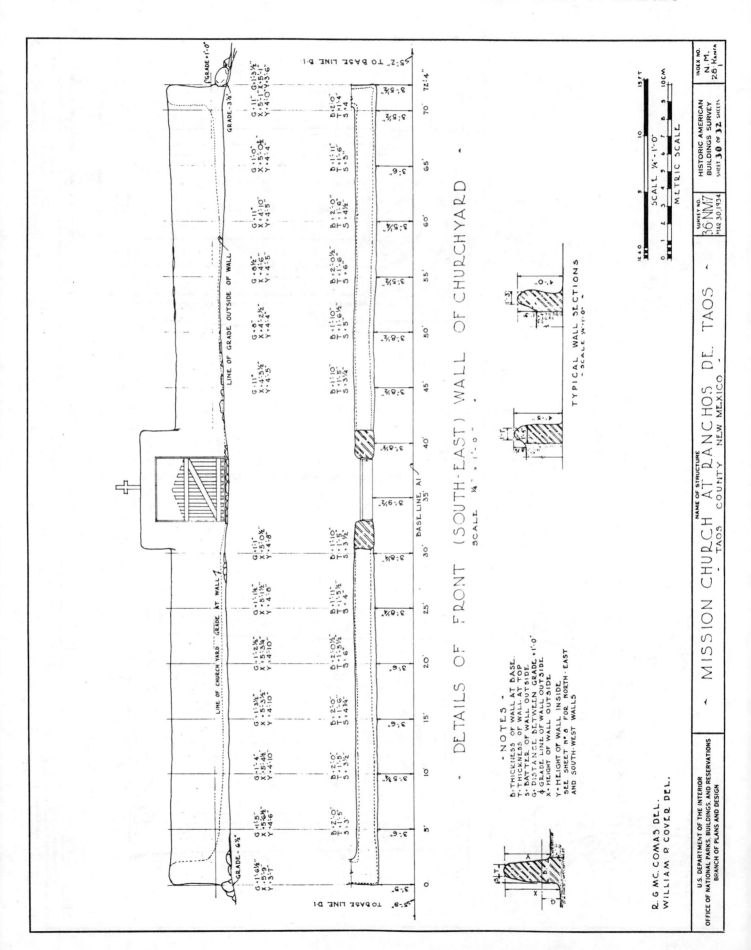

DETAILS OF FRONT (SOUTH-EAST) WALL OF CHURCHYARD

SCALE ¼" = 1'-0"

TYPICAL WALL SECTIONS

- NOTES -

B - THICKNESS OF WALL AT BASE.
T - THICKNESS OF WALL AT TOP
S - BATTER OF WALL OUTSIDE.
G - DISTANCE BETWEEN GRADE +1'-0"
$ - GRADE LINE OF WALL OUTSIDE
X - HEIGHT OF WALL OUTSIDE
Y - HEIGHT OF WALL INSIDE.
SEE SHEET No. 8 FOR NORTH-EAST
AND SOUTH-WEST WALLS

R. G. McCOMAS DEL.
WILLIAM R. COVER DEL.

U.S. DEPARTMENT OF THE INTERIOR
OFFICE OF NATIONAL PARKS, BUILDINGS, AND RESERVATIONS
BRANCH OF PLANS AND DESIGN

NAME OF STRUCTURE
MISSION CHURCH AT RANCHOS DE TAOS
- TAOS COUNTY NEW MEXICO -

SURVEY NO. 36 NM7
MAR 30, 1934

INDEX NO. N.M. 28 RANTA

HISTORIC AMERICAN BUILDINGS SURVEY
SHEET 30 OF 32 SHEETS.

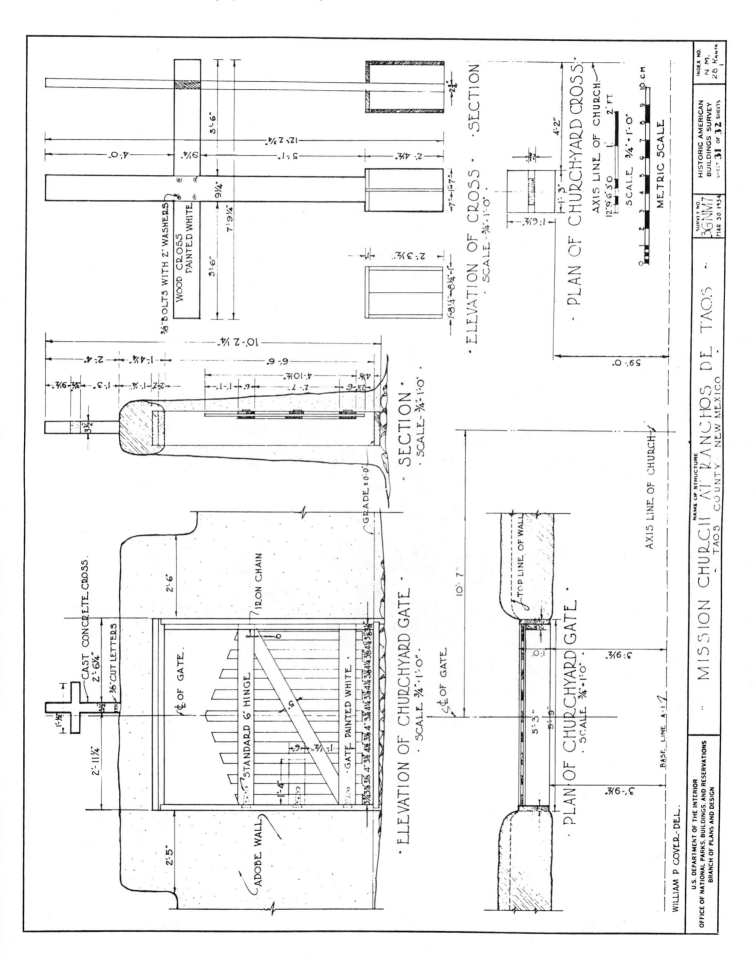

- COLOR STUDY OF REREDOS IN TRANSEPT -
SCALE 3/4"=1'-0"

WILLIAM P. COVER · DEL.

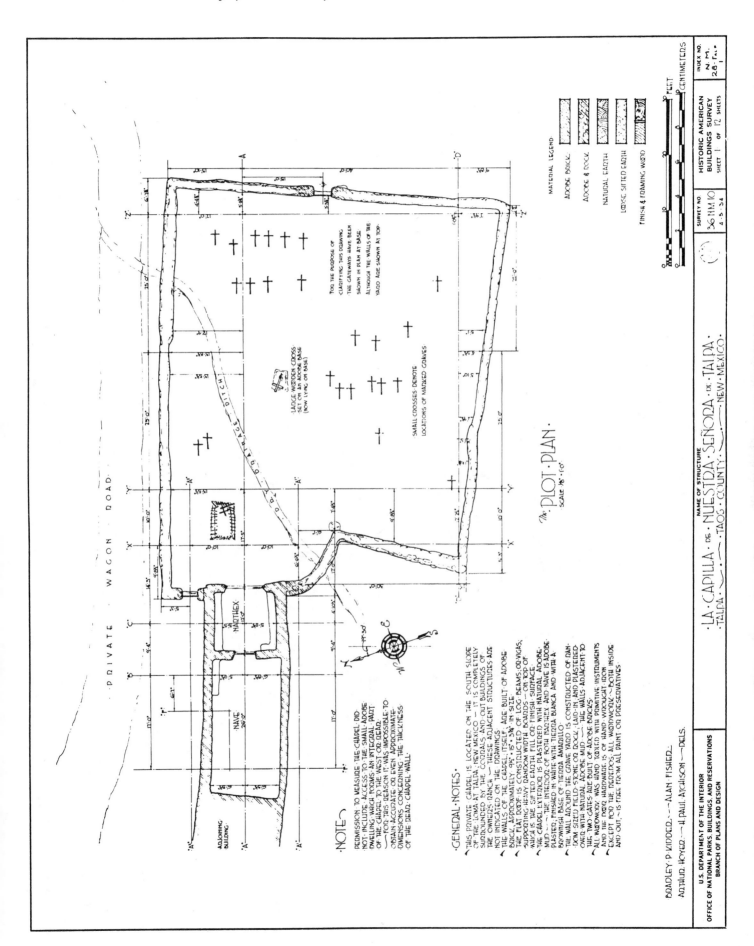

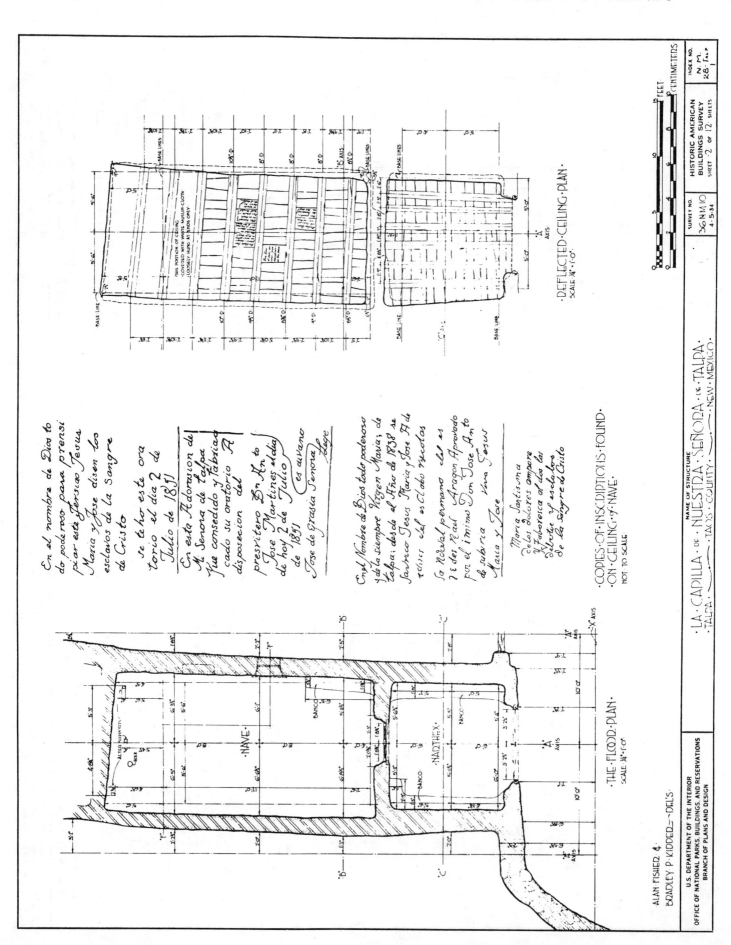

· DEFLECTED · CEILING · PLAN ·
SCALE ¼" = 1'-0"

En el nombre de Dios to
do poderoso para prensi
piar esta yglesia a Jesus
Maria y Jose disen los
esclavos de la Sangre
de Cristo

se te ho esta ora
torio el dia 2 de
Julio de 1851

En esta Adoracion de
M Senora de talpa
fue consedido y fabrica
cado su oratorio A
disposicion del

presvitero Dn Ano to
Jose Martines el dia
de hoy 2 de Julio
de 1851          es avano
Jose de Grasia Senora lage

Enel Nombre de Dios todo poderoso
y de la siempre Virgen Maria; de
talpa; desde el Año de 1838 se
fabrico Jesus Maria y Jose A la
rchise del es clabo viscolas

Sa Nidal pormano el es
li del Rael Aragon Aprovado
por el imimo Don Jose Anto
de subria   Viva Jesus
Maria y Jose

Maria Santisima
de los dolores ampare
y faboreica a todo las
Nortas y esclabos
de la Sangre de Cristo

· COPIES · OF · INSCRIPTIONS · FOUND ·
· ON · CEILING · OF · NAVE ·
NOT TO SCALE.

· NAVE ·

· NARTHEX ·

BANCO

BANCO

· THE · FLOOD · PLAN ·
SCALE ¼" = 1'-0"

ALAN FISHER &
BRADLEY P. KIDDER — DELS.

U.S. DEPARTMENT OF THE INTERIOR
OFFICE OF NATIONAL PARKS, BUILDINGS, AND RESERVATIONS
BRANCH OF PLANS AND DESIGN

NAME OF STRUCTURE
· LA · CAPILLA · DE · NUESTRA · SEÑORA · DE · TALPA ·
· TALPA · · TAOS · COUNTY · · NEW · MEXICO ·

SURVEY NO.
36 N.M. 10
4-5-34

HISTORIC AMERICAN
BUILDINGS SURVEY
SHEET · 2 · OF 12 SHEETS

INDEX NO.
N. M.
28 · F & P
1

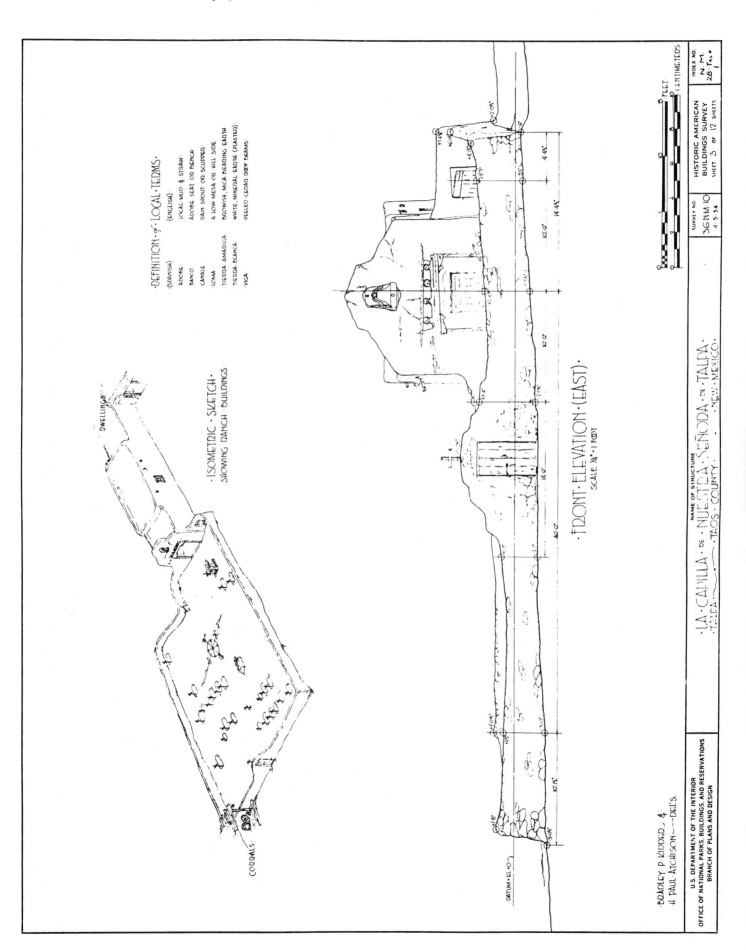

·DEFINITION · of · LOCAL · TERMS·

| (SPANISH) | (ENGLISH) |
|---|---|
| ADOBE | LOCAL MUD & STRAW. |
| BANCO | ADOBE SEAT OR BENCH. |
| CANALE | RAIN SPOUT OR SCUPPER. |
| LOMA | A LOW MESA OR HILL SIDE. |
| TIERRA AMARILLA | BROWISH, MICA BEARING EARTH |
| TIERRA BLANCA | WHITE, MINERAL EARTH (PLASTER) |
| VIGA | PEELED CEDAR ROOF BEAMS. |

·ISOMETRIC · SKETCH·
SHOWING RANCH · BUILDINGS

·FRONT · ELEVATION · (EAST)·
SCALE ¼" 1 FOOT

·LA · CAPILLA · DE · NUESTRA · SEÑORA · DE · TALPA·
·TALPA · — · TAOS · COUNTY · — · NEW · MEXICO·

BRADLEY P. KIDDER · &
H. PAUL · ATCHISON — DEL'S.

U.S. DEPARTMENT OF THE INTERIOR
OFFICE OF NATIONAL PARKS, BUILDINGS, AND RESERVATIONS
BRANCH OF PLANS AND DESIGN

SURVEY NO
36 NM 10
4-5-34

HISTORIC AMERICAN
BUILDINGS SURVEY
SHEET 3 OF 12 SHEETS

INDEX NO.
N. M.
28-TALP.
1

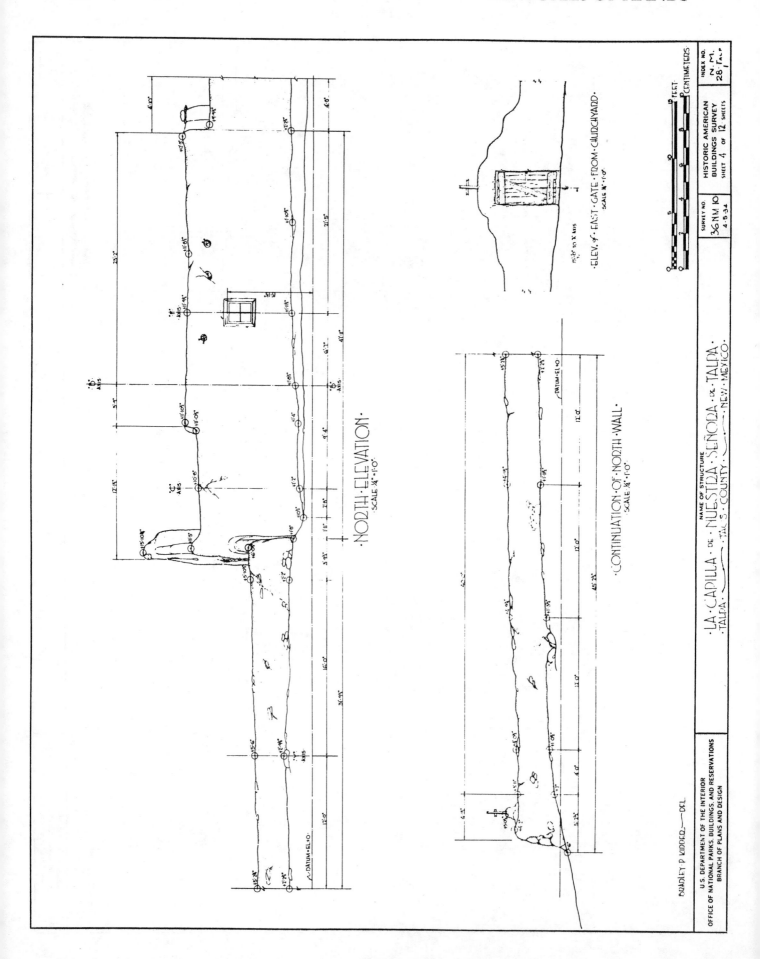

·NORTH·ELEVATION·
SCALE ¼"=1'-0"

·CONTINUATION·OF·NORTH·WALL·
SCALE ¼"=1'-0"

·ELEV·9·EAST·GATE·FROM·CHURCHYARD·
SCALE ¼"=1'-0"

NAME OF STRUCTURE
·LA·CAPILLA·DE·NUESTRA·SEÑORA·DE·TALPA·
·TALPA· ·TAOS·COUNTY· ·NEW·MEXICO·

U.S. DEPARTMENT OF THE INTERIOR
OFFICE OF NATIONAL PARKS, BUILDINGS, AND RESERVATIONS
BRANCH OF PLANS AND DESIGN

BRADLEY P. KIDDER——DEL.

SURVEY NO.
36 N.M. 10
4·5·34

HISTORIC AMERICAN
BUILDINGS SURVEY
SHEET 4 OF 12 SHEETS

INDEX NO.
N.M.
28·1

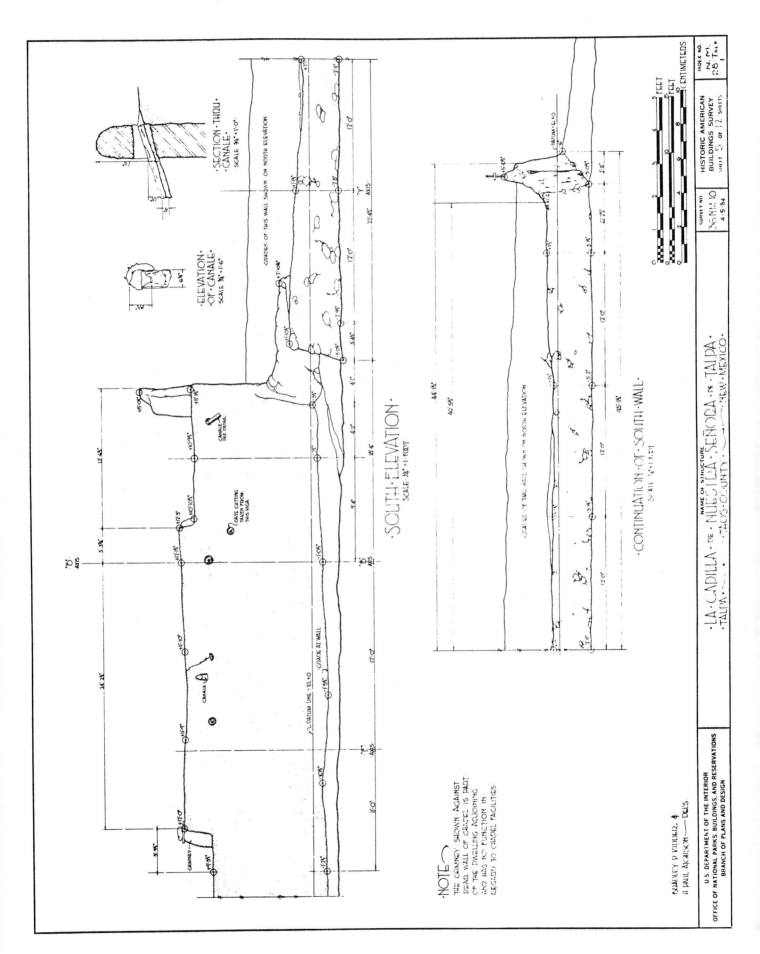

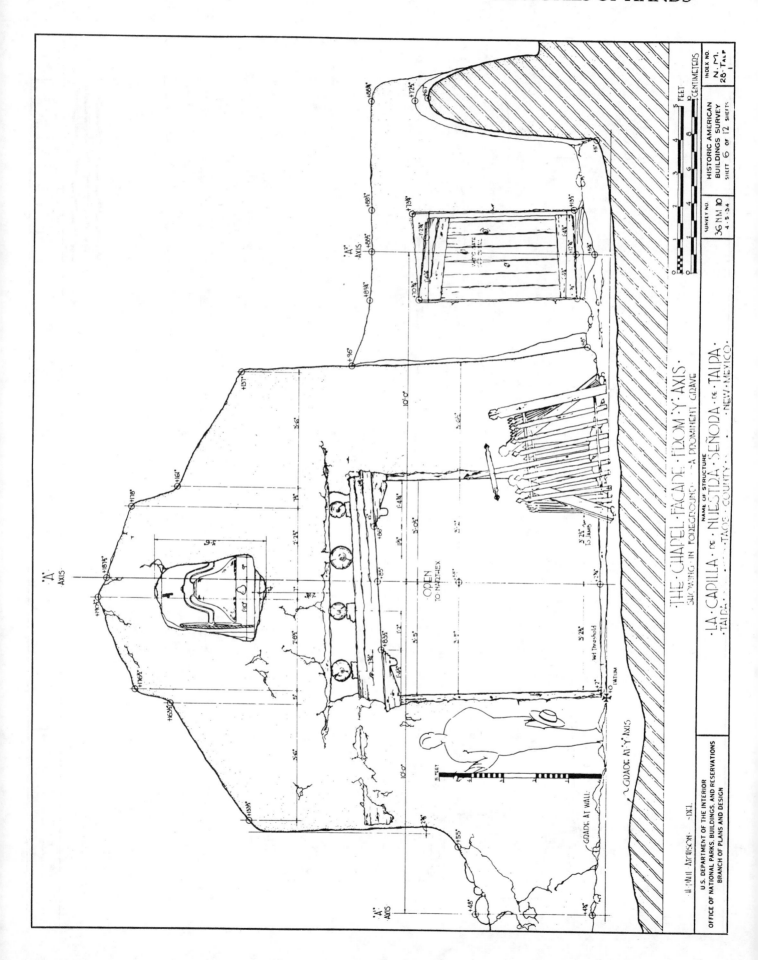

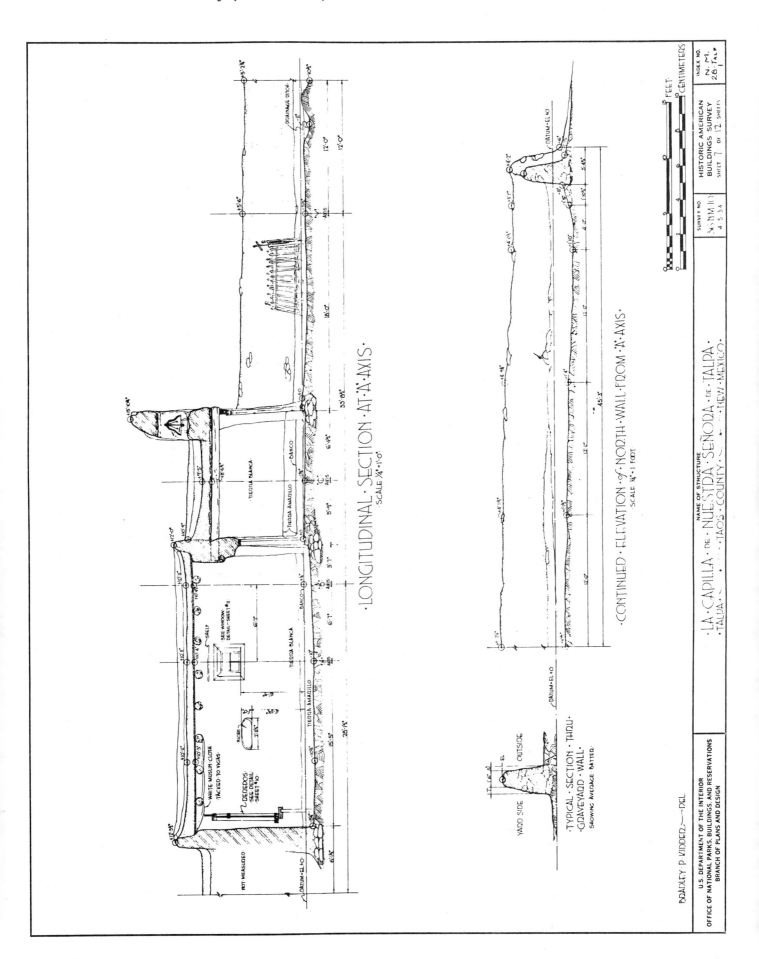

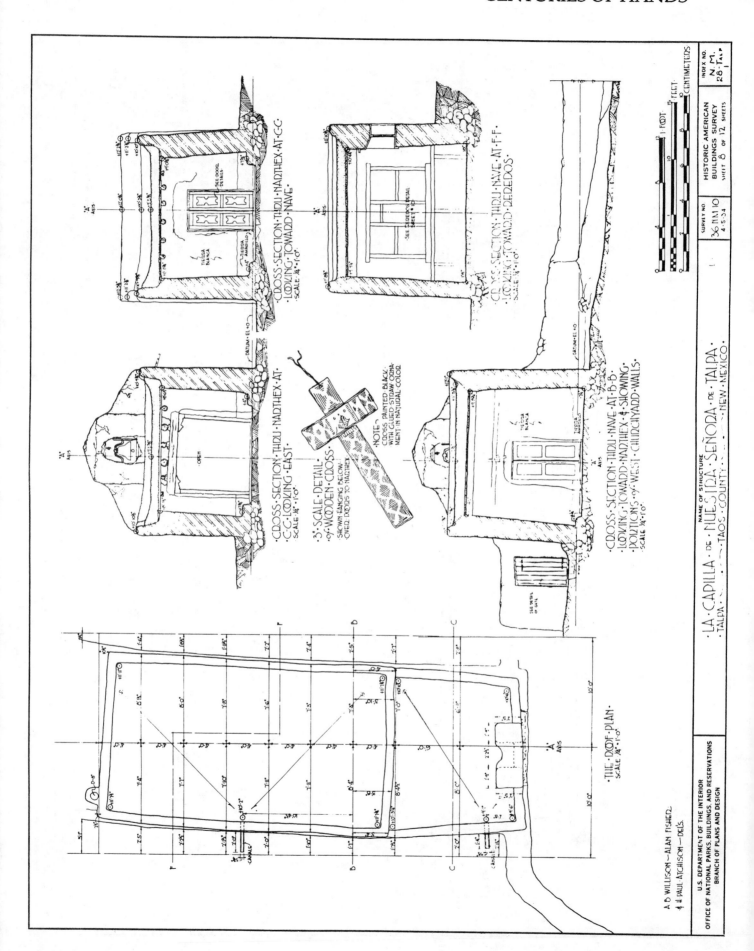

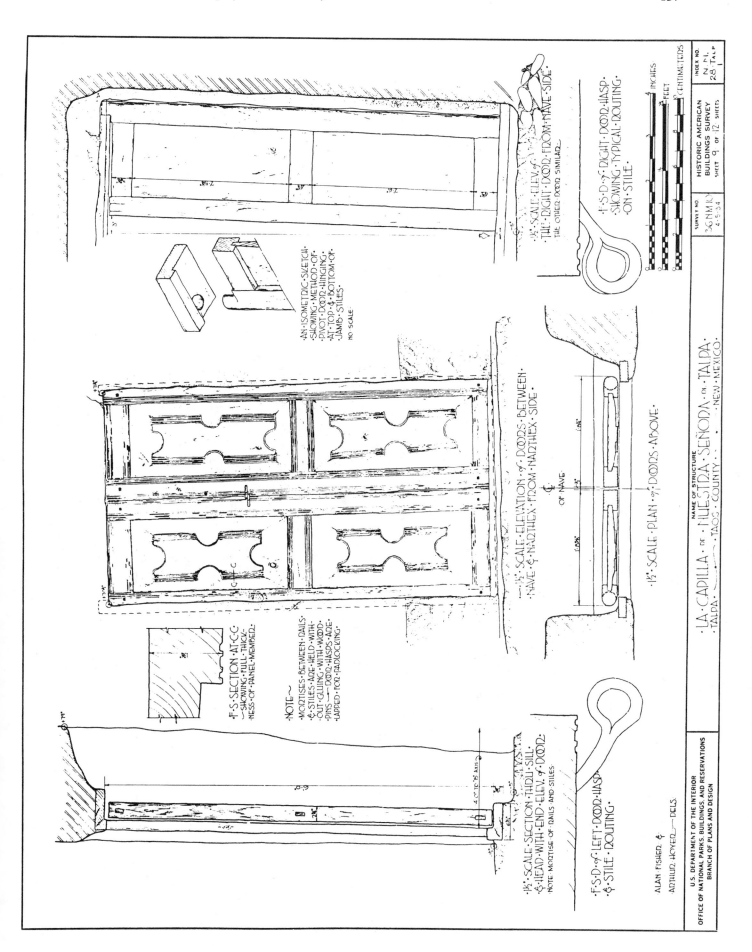

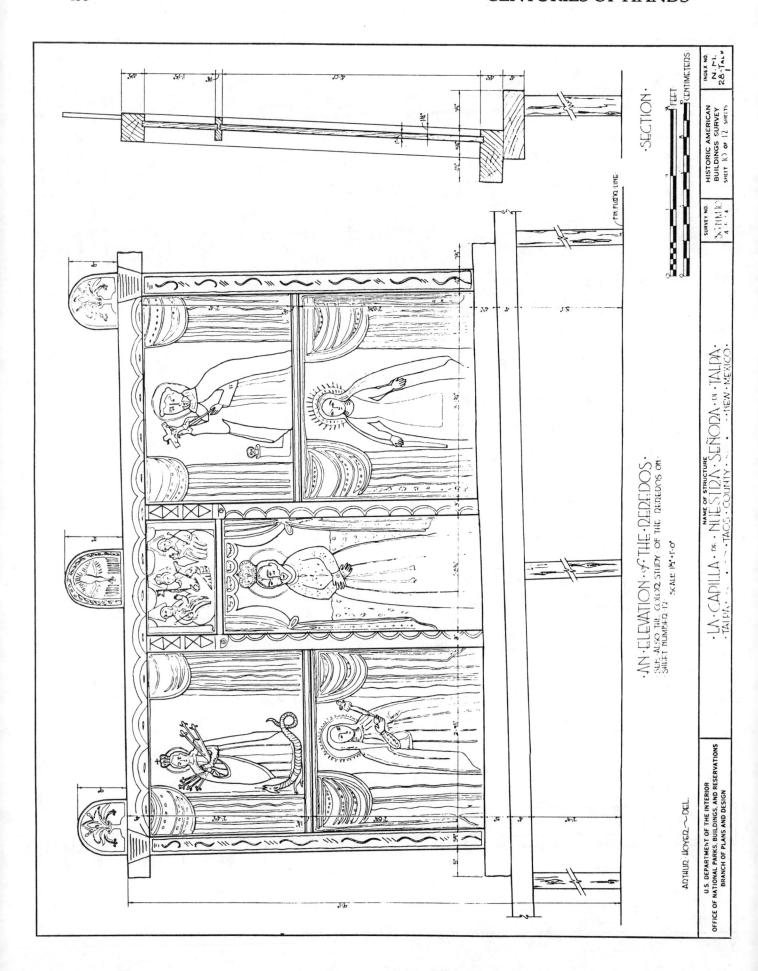

·AN·ELEVATION·of·THE·REREDOS·
SEE·ALSO·THE·COLOR·STUDY·OF·THE·REREDOS·ON·
SHEET·NUMBER·12    SCALE·½"·1'·0"

·SECTION·

ARTHUR·HOYER·DEL·

U.S. DEPARTMENT OF THE INTERIOR
OFFICE OF NATIONAL PARKS, BUILDINGS, AND RESERVATIONS
BRANCH OF PLANS AND DESIGN

NAME OF STRUCTURE
·LA·CAPILLA·DE·NUESTRA·SEÑORA·DE·TALPA·
·TALPA·    ·TAOS·COUNTY·    ·NEW·MEXICO·

SURVEY NO.
35·NM·10

HISTORIC AMERICAN
BUILDINGS SURVEY
SHEET 10 OF 12 SHEETS

INDEX NO.
N.M.
28-TALP

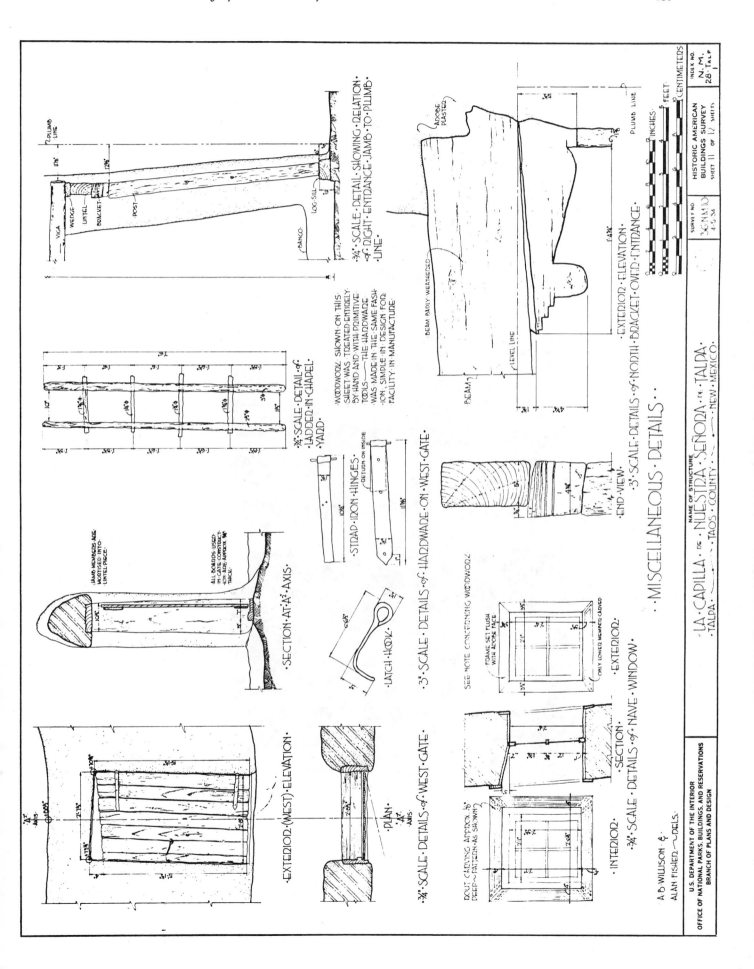

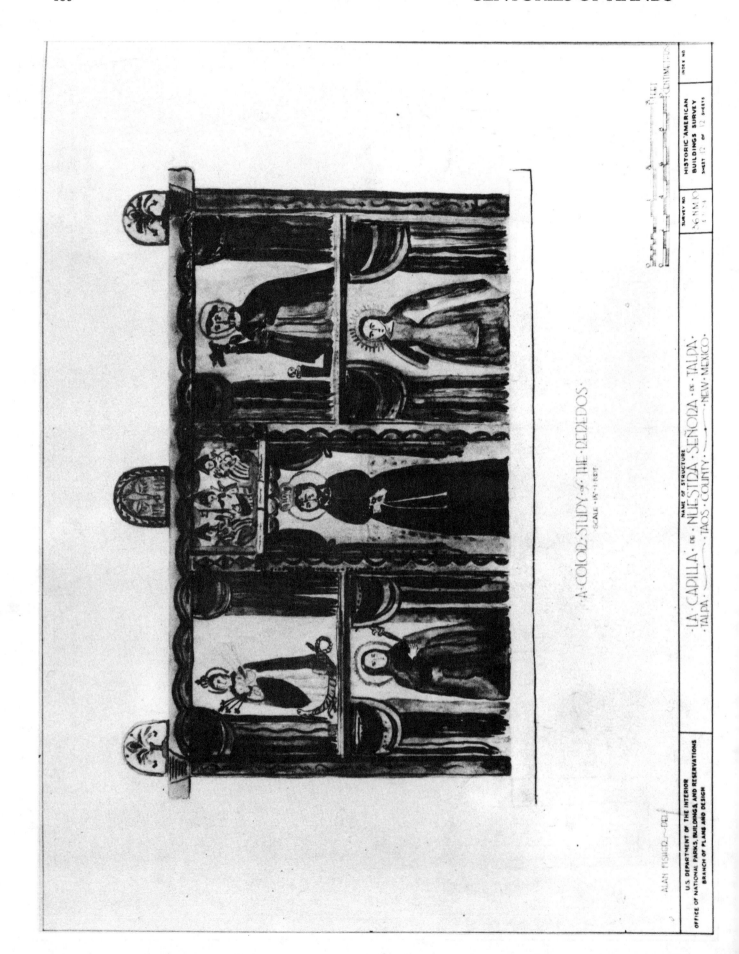

A·COLOR·STUDY·of·THE·REREDOS·
SCALE · 1/4" = 1 FEET

·LA·CAPILLA· de · NUESTRA·SEÑORA · de ·TALPA·
·TALPA· — ·TAOS·COUNTY· — ·NEW·MEXICO·